SECRET STAIRS
EAST BAY

A WALKING GUIDE
TO THE
HISTORIC STAIRCASES
OF BERKELEY AND OAKLAND

SANTA
MONICA
PRESS

Published by: Santa Monica Press LLC
P.O. Box 850
Solana Beach, CA 92075
1-800-784-9553
www.santamonicapress.com
books@santamonicapress.com

Printed in the United States

Santa Monica Press books are available at special quantity discounts when purchased in bulk by corporations, organizations, or groups. Please call our Special Sales department at 1-800-784-9553.

This book is intended to provide general information. The publisher, author, distributor, and copyright owner are not engaged in rendering professional advice or services. The publisher, author, distributor, and copyright owner are not liable or responsible to any person or group with respect to any loss, illness, or injury caused or alleged to be caused by the information found in this book.

ISBN-13 978-1-59580-063-3

Library of Congress Cataloging-in-Publication Data

Fleming, Charles.
 Secret stairs: East Bay : a walking guide to the historic staircases of Berkeley and Oakland / by Charles Fleming.
    p. cm.
 ISBN 978-1-59580-063-3
 1. Berkeley (Calif.)—Guidebooks. 2. Oakland (Calif.)—Guidebooks.
 3. Staircases—California—Berkeley—Guidebooks. 4. Staircases—California—Oakland—Guidebooks. 5. Historic sites—California—Berkeley—Guidebooks.
 6. Historic sites—California—Oakland—Guidebooks. 7. Walking—California—Berkeley—Guidebooks. 8. Walking—California—Oakland—Guidebooks.
 9. Berkeley (Calif.)—Buildings, structures, etc.—Guidebooks. 10. Oakland (Calif.)—Buildings, structures, etc.—Guidebooks. I. Title.
 F869.B5F55 2011
 917.94'6704—dc22
                          2011012117

Cover and interior design and production by Future Studio
Cover illustration and maps by Bryan Duddles
Photographs by Rita Harowitz

SECRET STAIRS
EAST BAY

A WALKING GUIDE
TO THE
HISTORIC STAIRCASES
OF BERKELEY AND OAKLAND

CHARLES FLEMING

CONTENTS

PART FOUR • OAKLAND: THE NORTH AND WEST

PART FIVE • EAST BAY & BEYOND

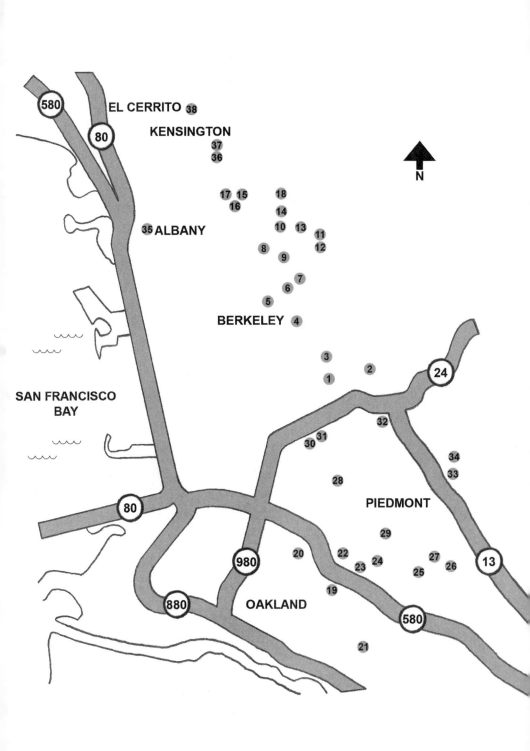

INTRODUCTION

The hills that rise above the communities of Berkeley and Oakland were developed in the early years of the 20th century. Accelerated by the terrible San Francisco earthquake and fire of 1906, when many homeowners fled their city to rebuild their homes and lives in the East Bay, the population of Berkeley tripled between 1900 and 1910. In the first three months after the earthquake, 30 new factories went up in Berkeley, and as many as 200,000 San Franciscans decamped for Oakland, almost quadrupling that city's population rolls.

Berkeley and Oakland were already connected to San Francisco, and to each other, by a rudimentary street car line. Inaugurated in 1903, the Key System ran electric traction trolley cars from Berkeley through Claremont, Piedmont, and Oakland, then across the bay—at first using a ferry, and later the lower half of the Bay Bridge—to San Francisco's Ferry Building. (The Berkeley–Oakland loop was the "head" of the key, the bridge its "shaft," and the ferry building its "teeth.") After 1906, to meet new demand, civic planners and real estate developers began building homes off the flatlands and into the hills, and extending the trolley lines up the canyons to serve them.

And in order to get the citizens up and down the hills from their new homes to those street cars, the developers built staircases.

More than a hundred years later, the street cars are gone. People have overcome their fear of San Francisco earthquakes, and made that city a greater metropolis than ever. The populations of Berkeley and Oakland and their surrounding East Bay neighbors have stopped growing. But the staircases remain, like forgotten pathways into history.

This book is intended as a guide to those pathways and that history. It is part travel book, part local color, and part exercise. The staircases rise out of the busier flatlands into the quieter hills, often going places where cars and their drivers can't go. Used as hiking trails, they offer the walker an off-the-beaten-track journey into the back roads, backyard East Bay, through neighborhoods that even longtime residents may not have explored. Because these neighborhoods are removed and somewhat remote, they have not been altered as much as their flatland counterparts. The old homes remain, often maintained

in their original condition. The hills are alive with hundred-year-old houses designed by well-known local architects like John Galen Howard, Henry Higby Gutterson, Bernard Maybeck, Julia Morgan, Leola Hall, and others.

The design of the walks in this book is inspired by the country "pub walk" books I first encountered in England and Ireland. Hyper-localized, set in little corners of County Kerry or West Kent, each slim volume contained a handful of hikes that

began and ended with a drink or a meal at a quiet roadside inn, separated by a long perambulation through the woods and fields. For a foreign visitor, each one felt a little like a wild goose chase, or a snipe hunt—cross the *stile,* look for a *kissing gate,* mind the *fingerpost,* and enter the *metalled tarmac path* leading to the *lychgate.* Every outing was an exercise in exercise and vocabulary, and returning safe and on time to the starting point was a real triumph.

The walks here are designed similarly, but without the linguistic challenges. Each "walk" describes a circular loop, beginning and ending at a café or public park, using the public stairways and walkways, linked together by lengths of public roadway, as its trails. Most take about an hour, though some are shorter or longer. Each is rated for difficulty—five for the most rigorous, one for the most casual—and has a stair count

CLAREMONT HOTEL, THE GRAND DAME OF THE EAST BAY HILLS.

indicating the number of actual staircase steps, and a distance figure indicating the total length of the walk. Each contains side notes identifying the architects who built the homes along the way, the developers who built the neighborhood, the famous event or personage connected to the names of the streets, and the marvels visible from the staircases. That's because almost every walk in the book includes, by geographic necessity, massive views: The staircases all rise in the East Bay hills, which rise from the plains, which rise from the bay. (Indeed, the original name of the original settlement that became Berkeley was "Ocean View.") From several points on several staircases on almost every walk in this book there are vistas of the San Francisco Bay, the Bay Bridge, the Golden Gate Bridge, the Port of Oakland, Alcatraz and Angel Island, Mount Tamalpais, Point Richmond, and more.

For simplicity's sake, this guide is broken into five geographic sections—two in Berkeley, two in Oakland, and one covering the northern communities of Albany, Kensington, and El Cerrito.

I had low expectations prior to the publication of *Secret Stairs: A Walking Guide to the Historic Staircases of Los Angeles*. I had walked alone for most of the three years I spent assembling that book, and had seldom met other walkers while I worked. Since the book's publication, though, I have met literally hundreds of stair-fans. Many of them have thanked me for introducing them to a side of Los Angeles they'd never known, and giving them a fresh, new, *healthy* way to experience their city. Their new-found interest in the stairs has brought new attention to an unheralded civic treasure. As a result, the public stairways of Silver Lake, Echo Park, Mt. Washington, Eagle Rock, Hollywood, Glassell Park, Pasadena, Santa Monica, and Pacific Palisades are now cleaner, safer, and more trafficked than at any time in the last several decades.

It is my hope that this book may find a similar audience and produce a similar result. But I have higher expectations, because many residents of Berkeley and Oakland, and the surrounding communities, are already hip to the fantastic network of public staircases lacing their hillsides. Indeed, I met more people walking the stairs of Berkeley in my first week of research on this book than I did in three years of research on its predecessor.

Their treatment of a visitor was unexpected, and encouraging. In Los Angeles, walking in some unfamiliar neighborhood, fumbling with map, notebook and pen, explaining my quest to a local homeowner, I was most often met with a *NIMBY*-minded response like, "You're not going to put *these* stairs in your book! We don't want people walking here!" In the hills of Berkeley and Oakland, similarly stumbling up and down the staircases with my stairwalking paraphernalia, I received an entirely different reaction. Upon hearing my intentions, one citizen after another said, "How wonderful! Have you found all of them already? There's a great one just around the corner." I met dozens of residents. Not one resident or homeowner tried to dissuade me.

This encourages me to believe that anyone using this book, anyone exploring and celebrating the stairs in a respectful way, will receive a similarly warm reception, and will enjoy the same pleasure I experienced walking the wonderful East Bay hills.

Those interested in further armchair exploration may find useful information at the following websites:

www.berkeleypaths.org
www.berkeleyheritage.com
www.oaklandurbanpaths.org
www.ectrailtrekkers.com
www.albanystrollroll.org
www.kensingtoncalifornia.org

Now, put on your boots and go.

OVERLEAF: THE CAL CAMPUS AND CAMPANILE.

PART ONE

BERKELEY:
THE SOUTH

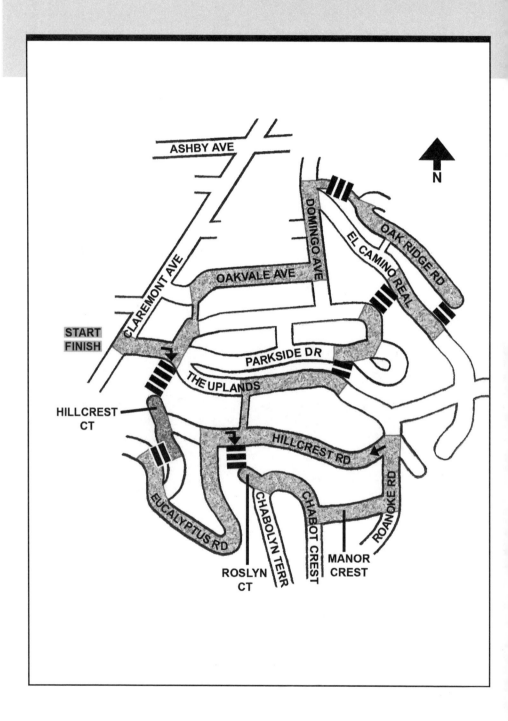

WALK #1

CLAREMONT: THE UPLANDS
DURATION: **1 hour, 15 minutes**
DISTANCE: **2.5 miles**
STEPS: **352**
DIFFICULTY: **3.5**
BUS: **49**

This is a lovely walk through a charming section of Claremont, featuring elegant homes, timeless views, and hidden staircases with curious names.

Start your walk where Berkeley and Oakland meet, in the shadow of the Claremont Resort, near the intersection of Ashby and Claremont Avenues. Have a coffee and biscotti at Semifreddi, known for its baked goods, at 3084 Claremont, or stop in next door at the charming Star Grocery, the market that time forgot.

Cross Claremont and enter The Uplands, flanked by massive stone gates and red-tile-covered bus benches. Walk straight ahead for a very short distance, admiring the enormous old homes. Then, just as you meet the first intersection, find The Footway on your right. This is a double-barreled staircase entrance, split by a steel railing, that climbs 36 steps to a sloping walkway.

Trudge up, noting as you go the fine shingle-sided home on your left. At the top, you arrive at the cul-de-sac end of Hillcrest Court, amidst a cluster of good-looking stucco Craftsman homes. Walk up the cul-de-sac until you are face-to-face with a baronial white mansion with a flagpole in the front yard—that would be the Claremont District Governor's home, if such a post existed.

Turn right and head slightly downhill, onto Hillcrest Road, noting the very fine home at 2 Hillcrest Court. Just ahead, past the big beige house at 85, find The Steps on your right.

These are, indeed, steps—65 of them, split by a handrail, dropping down sharply onto another stretch of Hillcrest Road. Turn left, and walk uphill. At the bend in the road, where Hillcrest doubles back, bear right onto Eucalyptus Road.

I didn't notice many eucalypti, but there are many fine Japanese maples, blazing in autumn, as you climb this slight rise. Off to your right you can hear and see Highway 24. Many homes here have the highway as their principal view—unfortunate.

In time you will meet Hillcrest once again. Turn right—observing a tennis court, which you don't often see in this area, across the street—and walk a short distance. Then, just after the house at 132, look to the right for South Crossways.

Drop down a delightful staircase—lovely and quiet, and according to the contractor's stamp, poured by Schnoor Bros.—falling 49 steps to land at the bulb end of Roslyn Court. Walk down this cul-de-sac, turn left onto Chabolyn Terrace, and follow it until it bends right and turns into Chabot Crest—perhaps named after Anthony Chabot, the engineer who in 1868 dammed Temescal Creek to create Oakland's first reservoir for drinking water. The reservoir is now known as Lake Chabot. With access off Broadway Terrace, it is also the starting point for Walk #31.

Chabot bends right and down. Turn left onto Manor Crest. The houses, lots, and landscaping here are more modest, but not without delights. Dig the chartreuse color scheme at 6729, and the whimsical pointed roof next door.

Manor Crest begins to climb, then meets Roanoke Road. Turn left and climb some more. (This is an exercise book. It's good for you.) Halfway up, note that you enter Berkeley, presumably leaving Oakland.

At the top of the hill, the houses become massive once

again. If you want to inspect a tiny, charming staircase that doesn't really lead anywhere, turn right onto Hillcrest. Walk a long block to the end of the road. On the left, find a short set of steps and a very private-feeling walkway leading you over to El Camino Real. It's a delightful shortcut, but…not for today.

Instead, turn left, onto Hillcrest again. Enjoy the shade of a line of giant pines, admiring the handsome shingle-sided homes at 220, 214, and 206, the Tudor-inspired beauty at 193, and the tiny funicular railway at 173.

Then, on your right, just after the house at 151, find The Crossways, the northern-running end of the South Crossways path you took a while ago. This one is a long, steep, bowling-alley of a walkway, descending through grand redwood shade to land back on The Uplands.

Turn right. Walk along, admiring the wide green belt of redwoods and pines on your left, and the enormous homes on your right. You're in the heart of The Claremont Uplands now. This is Berkeley's first "private residence park," created by the Mason-McDuffie company in 1905—the same year construction began on the nearby Claremont Hotel, though the hotel did not open until 10 years later. The big stone gates were designed by John Galen Howard—a local designer, and founder of UC Berkeley's architecture school. Howard was a supervising architect for the Cal campus master plan and designed many of its iconic structures, among them the famed Campanile, the Greek Theater, and Sather Gate. The neighborhood was served by a Key System electric trolley that ran straight down Claremont, all the way from the hotel to a terminus in San Francisco.

(Duncan McDuffie was a was a remarkable fellow. A Berkeley grad, he became interested in real estate and, with partner Mason, developed Berkeley's Northbrae section and San Francisco's St. Francis Wood. He spearheaded the mad idea to move the state capitol from Sacramento to Berkeley—see Walk #15 for details of *that* scheme. His own home was here in the Uplands; it featured gardens by two sons of Frederick Law Olmstead, the great landscape designer who drew the original plans for New York's Central Park and for the UC Berkeley campus. In addition to carving hillsides into homesteads, McDuffie was also a conservationist, and served as president of The Sierra Club from 1928 to 1931.)

Continuing along The Uplands, ignore the steps on the left just after the house at 90, but instead look for another set just after the house at 110. Cross the street and drop down the 31 steps across the green belt. You land on Parkside Drive. Turn right.

Ahead is a broad traffic circle, beautifully planted with ancient pine, oak, and palm. Turn left, just before the circle, onto The Plaza Drive. Then, just after the massive green and gray house at 99 (it's hard to find the number, but it's there), turn right onto The Cutoff.

This is a steeply sloping walkway that rises through a pair of lovely gardens and culminates in a sharp set of 25 steps up to El Camino Real. Cross the street, turn right, and enjoy a short stretch of flat street. It won't last long. Just after the garages attached to the house at 85, find Oakridge Steps.

This is your last steep climb, and it's a real climb—125 steps up, split by a steel handrail. Halfway up, stop to breathe and take in the vast views of Oakland, the city and its port, the Golden Gate Bridge to the west, and more. Then fight your way to the top.

You land on Oak Ridge Road. Turn left and walk along a flat section of street, catching glances of the grand view below. A friendly local fellow told me the whole hilltop area once was home to a wealthy timber baron. In time he sold out to developers Mason-McDuffie, who chopped his property into lots and built some of the homes that still stand today. (The brick house at 80, with its brick garage across the street, was built by a man who worked at the Port Costa brickworks, a turn of the century outfit based in the town of the same name.) As you walk on, watch for Park Path on your left, just after the house at 50. Don't take this. Instead, stop next door and, through the open garage, enjoy the view.

Continuing down Oak Ridge, as the road bends to the right, walk straight ahead. There, next to the big brown house at 34, drop down four steps and enter the sloping walkway that is Oakridge Path. Walk slowly, because there is a lot to see here. First, appreciate the profusion of bird life on your left, where ducks, geese, and chickens cluck at one another. Just across the way, check out the tile work at 22. Then, back to your left, note the sculptures behind the gate. A sign says you're welcome to walk inside, as long as you don't let the birds slip outside. The path winds down and around, and culminates in 17 steps down to Domingo Avenue. Turn left, cross El Camino Real again, and admire tiny Oak Park.

Across Domingo you might notice the opening to the continuation of Oakridge Path. It drops down to a creek, crosses it, and rises in the playground for John Muir School Park. That's a nice way to end your walk, but not as nice as the other way.

So walk straight ahead on Domingo, past the turning for Hazel Road, and then turn right onto Oakvale Avenue. There are oaks here, but mostly there are liquidambars, quite old and, in autumn, afire with color. Descend a gentle slope, admiring the lovely low-eaved cottage at 41 and the gorgeous redwoody garden next door. At 35, turn in slightly to take a quick look at a bend in Claremont Creek, helpfully identified by a charming hand-painted sign on the creek bank.

The road jogs to the left to accommodate the little river. You cross a stone bridge, and find the creek now on your left. Follow along, past a beautiful brick-and-board house at 18, and past a collection of log-cabin garages. Just after these, turn left onto Encina Walk, which will carry you over the creek and onto the driveway of the house belonging to those log-cabin garages.

The driveway will deposit you on The Plaza again. Turn right, taking time to admire the elegant old home on the left at 35, and the broad gardens attached to 6 and 10 on the right. Turn the corner onto The Uplands, noting the Colonial white charmer at 9, which you will see is reached by a cobble-stoned bridge over another section of Claremont Creek.

Just ahead, pass again through the large stone gates. Across the street is your starting point.

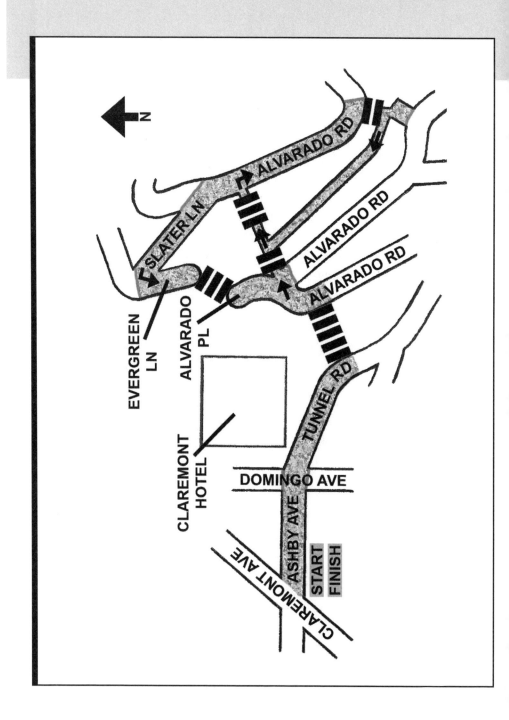

WALK #2

CLAREMONT HOTEL HEIGHTS
DURATION: **1 hour**
DISTANCE: **1.6 miles**
STEPS: **544**
DIFFICULTY: **3.5**
BUS: **49**

This is a short walk with steep staircases and heavenly views, and includes a tour of the historic Claremont Hotel Resort and Spa, and some fine dining options.

Start your walk near the intersection of Ashby and Claremont Avenues, at the foot of the monumental bright-white façade of the Claremont Hotel, perhaps with a "crispy" from Fournée Bakery at 2912 Domingo Avenue, or a hearty breakfast next door at Rick and Ann's. Finish off with a short tour of the hotel. Its massive reception lobby is filled with historic photographs of the area, and features a baby grand player-piano. When you're done with that, head for the bottom of the parking lot entrance from Tunnel Road. On the uphill side, just east of the guard gate and the parking lot, find your first staircase hidden in the bushes on the hill.

This is Short Cut, a bower of shade over 10 stone steps, a stone walkway, and 35 more stone steps (with a fine stone bench halfway up) that deposits you on Alvarado Road. Bear slightly left, and walk a half-block to where Alvarado Road meets Alvarado Place. Directly ahead, you'll find Eucalyptus Path. Grab a handrail and start climbing.

This is a true walk-street. The houses on it cannot be reached in any way except up the steps. The days I've walked there, I've met women carting groceries, women carting infants, and women carting infants *and* groceries.

Climb 139 steps to the top, pausing in the middle to admire the towering views of the Claremont, the Berkeley flats, the bay and Bay Bridge, and even sections of the Port of Oakland. Note too, halfway up, a pathway leading off to your right. This is Sunset Trail, which you'll learn more about in a little while. Continue climbing, past the big redwood bungalows in the Leola Hall style, to land at 678 Alvarado Road. Notice the trash can funicular railway at 688; it helps, on a hill like this.

Turn right and head downhill, past the massive newer homes that populate this side of the mountain. Many of these are new homes because the old ones burned in the terrible 1991 Oakland firestorm. The catastrophic burn started as a grass fire less than a mile from here. Diablo winds blew the fire across the hillsides. The non-native eucalyptus trees went up like Roman candles. More than 3,500 homes in the Oakland and Berkeley hills were destroyed, and 25 lives were lost to the conflagration. Curiously, however, some lives and homes were saved by *these staircases*. Residents who could not evacuate down the narrow windy roads, crowded with fleeing homeowners and arriving emergency vehicles, escaped using the stairways. Firefighters who could not get up the crowded roads brought hoses up the stairs.

Continue down Alvarado. Just after the house at 277, on your right, find charming Willow Walk. These are old stairs, with newish railings, that drop 51 steps and a sloping walkway into a deep overhang of welcome shade, to drop you at the southern end of Sunset Trail. For now, pass this by, dropping down an additional 27 stone steps through the dense redwood forest to land back on Alvarado Road. Enjoy the little creek and park here, fitted with benches, before turning back to Willow Walk and climbing up again. Walk the 27 steps up to the unusual intersection of Walk and Trail, and turn left onto the pathway.

(For an amusing side-trip, continue past the little park and turn left onto Alvarado Road. Follow it up a slight grade as it bends around and meets Vicente Road. Turn right onto Vicente. A little way along, just after the house at 146, find a private-looking wooden stairway on the left. Climb up! At the top is Vicente Canyon Hillside, a 2.5-acre pocket park studded with trees and trails. When you've enjoyed this lovely secret spot, return down Vicente to Alvarado, turn left, and find the bottom of Willow Walk again. Turn right up the hillside, and resume the walking directions below.)

This is a long flat walkway along a trail that separates upper and lower Alvarado. There are occasional benches on the left and occasional views on the right as the path winds through some old-growth oak and redwood, passing the backyards of the large houses on either side. One has built itself a redwood viewing platform. Another has made a fence of wire, not redwood, so you can better enjoy the views. (One or two other backyards may contain barking dogs.)

In time, meet Eucalyptus Path once more. Turn right and head up the stairs again, climbing only 82 steps this time to land again on upper Alvarado. Turn left, this time, and walk to the corner. Here you meet Slater Lane. Turn left, descend to where Slater meets Evergreen Lane, and turn left again. At the bottom of the cul-de-sac, when you can walk no more, find Evergreen Path. This is a stately, elegant walkway, fitted with handrails, that drops in mathematical harmony down eight matching sets of 16 steps each, for a total of 128.

You land just behind the Claremont Hotel. Take the brushy pathway to your left, and follow this a hundred feet or so to Alvarado Place. Pick up the asphalt here, and walk to the corner. Turn right, onto Alvarado Road, and immediately find Short Cut again on your left. Descend the 45 steps back to the hotel driveway, and return to your starting point.

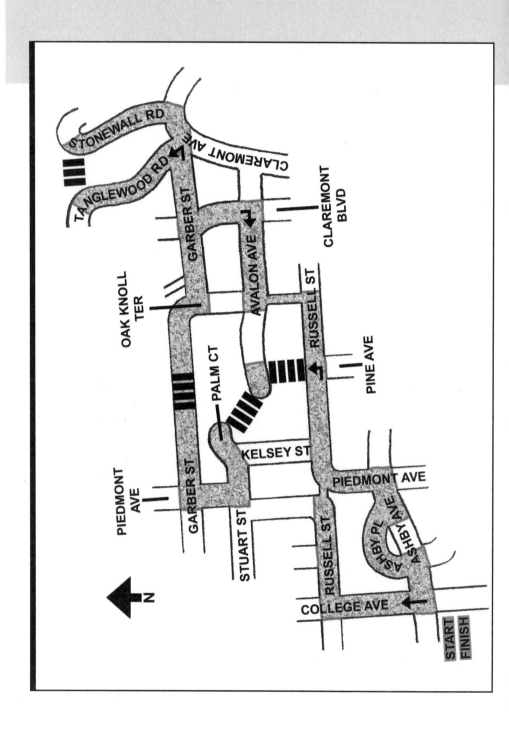

WALK #3

ELMWOOD PARK
DURATION: **1 hour**
DISTANCE: **2.5 miles**
STEPS: **159**
DIFFICULTY: **2**
BUS: **604, 605, 851, 51B**

This is a gentle walk though an architectural gold mine of fascinating houses, including signature works by designers Julia Morgan and Leola Hall. Despite its former "whites-only" status, and current elegance, the district was once home to political radicals like Jane Fonda, Tom Hayden, and Eldridge Cleaver.

Begin your walk in the Elmwood section of southeastern Berkeley, near the intersection of Ashby and College Avenues, perhaps with an ice cream from justifiably popular Ici, at 2948 College, or a coffee and deli sandwich at Italian grocer A.C. Ferrari at 2905. Check out also Mrs. Dalloway's, a fine bookstore specializing in gardening titles, and the pleasant Elmwood Café, both also on College.

When you've satisfied all your appetites, begin walking north on College. Turn right at the first corner, onto Russell Street, and walk past a substation of the Berkeley Fire Department and Nabolom, one of the city's few vegan bakeries.

Already you have left the bustle of the little Elmwood commercial district and are in a quiet, leafy neighborhood. The walk begins with charming, unpretentious houses. Note the fine garden at 2734, and the handsome elderly Craftsman at 2746. At the corner of Piedmont, you may stop to read a plaque describing Kelsey Ranch, the original owners of this tract of land, and the folks who planted the elm trees that gave the district its name.

Press on. Far ahead you will see the stark white façade of the Claremont Hotel, the vast tennis-club-and-spa resort that opened in 1915, and has been a destination ever since. (It used to be an electric rail terminus. Trains from Oakland came directly to its door, on tracks running up the driveway that now separate the hotel from the tennis courts.) Nearer by, appreciate the fine pink Mission Revival-style edifice at 2827—a Henry Lawrence Wilson Mission Revival home—and the hideaway cottage next door at 2829.

Walk on, then turn left where you meet Pine Avenue, just before the big trio of redwood trees at 2901. This is Pine Path, and your first staircase. It begins with a gently sloping walkway, and culminates in an elegant, if elderly, climb of 51 steps whose contractor's stamp bears the name of James E. Wentworth of Oakland.

You land at 2900 Avalon Avenue. Turn left, and begin to notice the first of this walk's really big houses, a grab-bag of architectural styles, including handsome structures at 2905 and 2909. Follow the sidewalk along and, just after the house at 2904, turn left onto Avalon Walk. (A handy sign on the left warns you to beware of "Dogs in Yard." But you will already know this, because they'll already be barking.)

This is another elegant stairway, curved at the top and offering handrails, that drops 44 steps down to Palm Court. Walk straight ahead, eschewing the left-hand turn onto Kelsey Street, to Piedmont.

Here at the corner, pause to admire the home at 2800 Piedmont. This is the work of Leola Hall—along with homes down the block at 2758, 2754, and 2752, and around the next corner, all along Stuart Street. Known as the "girl architect of Berkeley," despite her political work as a crusading suffragette, Hall built at least a dozen of her signature Craftsman bungalows in a single year: 1909. Her homes featured small kitchens and bedrooms, large public spaces—Hall liked entertaining but not cooking, it was said—and a profligate use of bare wood and glass.

When you've absorbed enough of that, turn right onto Piedmont, walk one block to the elementary school, past its lush vegetable gardens, and turn right again, this time onto Garber Street.

Garber—named after a prominent Berkeley-area judge who owned much of the land in this neighborhood, and after whom the large park farther up Claremont is also named—runs past a series of pleasant stucco bungalows up to a peculiarity: A winding paved driveway heading uphill, but gated against car traffic, flanked with pedestrian walkways on both sides. Stay to the left, and take a series of 50 stairs up to the top, under an incongruous blend of redwood, royal palm, elm, and sycamore trees. This is Garber Path. A contractor's stamp near the top risers indicates the stairs were poured in 1928.

Walk on as Garber descends past increasingly stately homes. Pay particular attention to the Chelsey Bonestell House at 2915—a twin-chimneyed delight—and to the four houses by Henry Gutterson, running from 2922 down to 2904. Gutterson himself lived at 2922.

Garber arrives shortly at the delightful and delightfully named Monkey Island Park, given that title because of a large monkey tree planted there when the park was built as part of a traffic-calming scheme. The tree is now gone, but so is the traffic. Enjoy the good shade and welcome bench here, then cross the park and continue on Garber. Enjoy a profusion of hydrangeas, on the left-hand side of the street and then use the crosswalk to cross busy Claremont Boulevard. Ignore the "No Outlet" signs dead ahead—those are for *cars*; more of that traffic-calming scheme—and continue on Garber. Here the homes are larger still and less unpretentious. At the "T" intersection ahead, fitted with barriers against automobile traffic, turn left into quiet Tanglewood Road.

Here you will find delightful homes, old and new, like the Ernest Coxhead at 28 and the Walter Ratcliff Jr. at 22. Hawks whirl and keen overhead from their nesting places in Claremont Canyon, high on the hills above you. Admire the fine solarium and noble stone lions at 18—a home designed by J. A. Marshall, developer of much of the surrounding property. Then, just past the house at 3 Tanglewood, where the road curves to the left, find your next staircase on the right.

This is Tanglewood Path, and it's not tangled at all. Instead, it rises six steps to a long sloping cement walkway, which climbs 100 yards or so through deep shade to eight more steps and a continuing slope. On the left, you brush against the Clark Kerr Campus, a division of UC Berkeley, named after the economics professor who became UC Berkeley's first chancellor. (The buildings in this wooded area now provide housing for international students and faculty, and were once the campus of the California School for the Deaf and Blind, a legendary institution that occupied this location from 1869 to 1980.) As you land at the top of the path, this gives onto the Claremont Canyon Regional Preserve, a forest of eucalyptus trees and a maze of hiking trails.

For now, turn around to enjoy the Golden Gate Bridge views behind you, and head downhill onto Stonewall Road. You'll pass new homes and old oaks, and descend gently. At the bottom of the hill, pause to admire the fine Greene and Greene-style Craftsman, with koi pond, at 1 Stonewall.

Then turn right onto noisy Claremont Avenue. Walk a short block, and turn right again back onto Tanglewood, and then left at once past the barriers onto Garber. Walk one last block of Garber, enjoying the fine heavy shade, and turn left at the first corner onto Claremont Boulevard. (Ahead you will see two pillars, part of the gate that used to span the roadway and enclose the exclusive Claremont area. Several sets of these pillars still exist, though the gates are gone.) Huge homes preside. Note the remarkable brick confection at 2815—a T. Paterson Ross home from 1910—and its next door neighbor at 2821—a fine Julia Morgan from 1928, with an elegant Art Nouveau design around the entrance.

Cross Claremont carefully at the first corner, and turn onto Avalon Avenue. Enjoy the Art Deco window glass at 2967, a 1909 home from architect Edward Seely, and the Spanish Colonial Revival at 2957, another Walter Ratcliff Jr. Continue as Avalon rises slightly to meet Oak Knoll Terrace. There, on the far left side, just after the house at 2838, find the almost-hidden Oak Knoll Path.

This is a sloping walkway, like a wide sidewalk, that descends narrowly between the grand houses and two imposing brick columns. Pass through these and turn right onto Russell Street once again. Walk straight on, pausing to admire the enormous brick-and-wood mansion at 2911, taking particular note of the extension—reached by a bridge over the driveway—and the fine selection of royal palms. This enormous home was built in 1908 by D. J. Patterson, who also designed the old Berkeley train station building. Since 1966, the structure housed the Judah L. Magnes Museum of Jewish Art and Life, a magnificent collection of art and artifacts that is currently being moved to a new downtown Berkeley facility on Allston, which will be open to the public in fall 2011.

At Pine, you'll pass the entrance to your first staircase. A long block further on, turn left onto Piedmont, and then turn right at the first corner onto Ashby Avenue. Bear right, onto Ashby Place, to find a few more interesting older homes, including the handsome one at 2733—a Julia Morgan-Ira Hoover gable-roofed home from 1908.

Turn right, where Ashby Place meets Ashby Avenue, and walk one block. You're back at College, and your starting point.

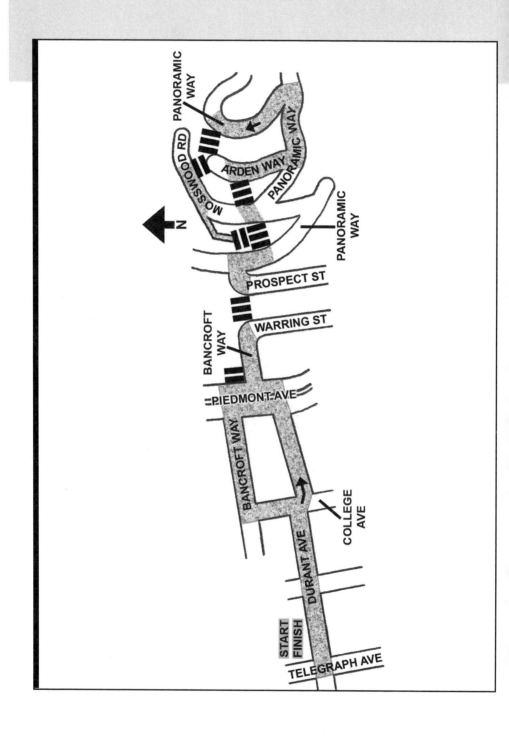

WALK #4

PANORAMIC HILLS
DURATION: **1 hour**
DISTANCE: **2 miles**
STEPS: **504**
DIFFICULTY: **3–3.5**
BUS: **51, 49**

This is a relatively short walk with some relatively steep staircases, through lovely shaded neighborhoods and past some classic Berkeley architecture—and featuring, of course, panoramic views. It is to be avoided on Cal "game days," when the massive influx of football fans makes parking and driving a tactical challenge.

Begin your walk just south of the UC Berkeley campus, near the corner of Durant Avenue and Telegraph Avenue, perhaps with a frankfurter from famous Top Dog at 2534 Durant Avenue. Thus fortified, begin walking east on Durant, past the Durant Hotel (a 1928 construction from designer William H. Weeks) and the first of this walk's many redwood trees, sloping up toward the Berkeley hills. You'll pass the former home of the Berkeley Art Museum on the left, and then walk another block before you cross the street and turn left onto Piedmont Avenue.

This is the beginning of the university's fraternity row. At 2307 is Thorsen House, a marvel of Southern California's Arts and Crafts architects Charles and Henry Greene. This understated 1908 masterpiece, one of the last of the great wooden houses built by the Pasadena-based designers, now houses the fraternity Sigma Chi.

Just past this charming building, turn right onto Bancroft
Way, and walk up one long block. To your left is International
House, the residential dorm originally intended for foreign stu-
dents, paid for by John D. Rockefeller and designed by George
W. Kelham—known also for the Federal Reserve Building in
San Francisco and several on-campus buildings nearby, among
them the Gothic, castle-like Bowles Hall, a men's undergradu-
ate dormitory.

Dead ahead, where Bancroft meets Warring Street, is
your first staircase—Bancroft Steps. This is a wide walkway, 13
steps at the bottom and 11 at the top, with a sloping walkway

A classic East Bay park.

in between. There is a good handrail, and where the asphalt is worn away you can see the original brick pavement below.

At the top, cross the parking lot (noting the stately Cal football stadium to your left), cross Prospect Street, and turn right into Panoramic Way. About 100 feet in, beneath an overhang of oak trees, you'll find your next staircase rising on the left.

This is the lovely Orchard Lane staircase, designed by Henry Atkins for the original Panoramic Hill developer Warren Cheney. (Cheney was a journalist, lawyer, and realtor who had once been editor of the literary journal *The Californian*. The original "orchard" was a collection of almond trees.) Identified on a plaque partway up the stairs as "one of Berkeley's romantic treasures," it's a wide, stately set, rising 33 steps to an intersection of two pedestrian avenues. Stop to appreciate the elderly concrete benches, and evidence of an old fountain, before bearing right and up into the next set of stairs. Climb 79 steps over several stages, gathering increasingly impressive views as you go, to land at the intersection of Panoramic Way and Mosswood Road.

The Orchard Lane steps continue. To find them, jog slightly left and then slightly right, following the bend in Panoramic. Then climb again, starting on the left, just after the house at 101. (This house, like the ones lining Orchard Lane and many others in this district, is the work of architect Walter Steilberg. He is known, and his homes can be recognized, by the use of glazed Chinese tiles in a particular color of teal-green. Steilberg was employed as an engineer by the more famous Julia Morgan, and is also known for his patent of a building material called Fabricrete, which employed a fire-proof concrete.) Rise up 158 steps, over many stages, shaded by pine and palm, and land panting just opposite 62 Arden Road.

Turn right and head down this shady lane, keeping an eye out for wildlife. The first time I walked these steps was a hot September afternoon, and I encountered a fine-looking stag, with an impressive four-point rack of antlers, munching grass on the hillside. At the bottom of the hill, turn left onto Panoramic, and climb some more. Here you will find wood-shingled homes, clinging to the hillsides, and big oak trees interrupting marvelous views of the San Francisco Bay.

Take the hairpin left at the first intersection, remaining on Panoramic, and climbing uphill. (If you have the time and energy for a longer walk, and would like to add 15 to 20 minutes to this one, skip the hairpin turn onto Panoramic and continue instead straight ahead onto Dwight Way. Pass a right-hand turning for Dwight Place, and a left-hand turning for another stretch of Panoramic. Continue along, without turning, as Dwight undergoes a name change and becomes Panoramic. Follow Panoramic until you come to a substantial fork in the road. Take the left-most side of the fork. Walk until you run out of pavement, and continue straight ahead onto a wide trail. This will lead you, in time, back to Panoramic. When you hit pavement again, turn right onto Panoramic and watch for the Arden stairs on your right.) Trek up Panoramic, enjoying the big views. After five minutes or so, just past a water reservoir buried in the hillside to your left, you'll find the next stairs.

This is Arden Path, which begins with 33 big wooden stairs and leads to a sloping pathway, well shaded and winding between lovely redwood-sided homes, and drops a final 7 steps down to the intersection of Arden Path, Arden Road, and Arden Steps. Note the fine big home here at 100 Arden (a clinker-brick-and-wood structure from 1915), then take a hard right and head down the Arden Steps. (You might have already noticed that some of the staircases are marked with a bright gold and blue "stair" graphic, bearing the name of the staircase and the direction in which it goes. These are the handiwork of a long-time local resident named Richard White, who designed them to assist people who might be using the stairs in an emergency. He and other members of the Panoramic Hill Association's Emergency Preparedness Committee posted the signs all over their neighborhood. I found them extremely welcome.) These drop down a steep 101 steps and land opposite 37 Mosswood

Road. Turn left, and follow Mosswood as it winds downhill.

Just after the big house at 21 Mosswood—which features some elements by John Hudson Thomas, the famed Bay Area architect who studied under John Galen Howard and Bernard Maybeck at Cal, and who went on to design literally dozens of homes in the Berkeley and Oakland hills—you'll find the entrance to Mosswood Lane. (For a little architectural treat, walk on a bit. The next house on your right is a Frank Lloyd Wright Jr. "Usonian" house, designed by Wright in 1939, but not built until 1974, after his death.) Turn right into this narrow corridor, and follow the path between the houses and along the line of stately redwood trees down and to the left. In time, you pass a lovely wooden bench on the left and, on the right, the Fabricrete and green-tile home that Walter Steilberg built for himself.

Just after, you'll drop down 12 steps and find yourself back at the intersection of Mosswood Lane and the Orchard Lane steps. Turn right, take the 33 steps back to Panoramic, turn right, cross Prospect and the parking lot, and walk down the 24 final Bancroft steps. (For another quick architectural sidestep, take the steps back down to Panoramic, then turn left, and walk up. At 23, you'll see one of Berkeley's many Bernard Maybeck homes—the so-called Boke House—a fine "Swiss Chalet" style home from 1901.)

For an alternate route back, turn right where Bancroft meets Piedmont, take five steps down to the crosswalk and cross the street in front of International House, and continue downhill on Bancroft. You'll pass Berkeley's law school on your right, and a series of stately homes turned frat houses on your left. The fine-looking building that houses Adagia restaurant was designed for the Presbyterian Church by famed local architect Walter Ratcliff Jr. It was redesigned to make room for Adagia in 2003, but is still owned by the church.

At the corner of College, stop for a fresh lemonade or pick-me-up coffee at Strada before returning to your starting point.

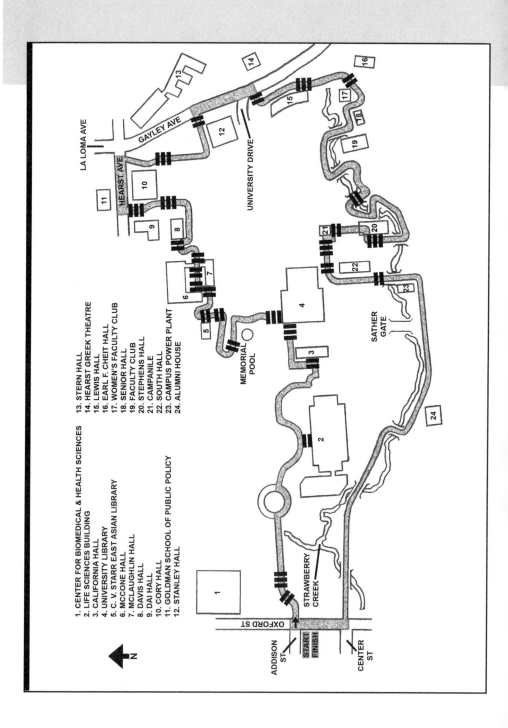

1. CENTER FOR BIOMEDICAL & HEALTH SCIENCES
2. LIFE SCIENCES BUILDING
3. CALIFORNIA HALL
4. UNIVERSITY LIBRARY
5. C. V. STARR EAST ASIAN LIBRARY
6. MCCONE HALL
7. MCLAUGHLIN HALL
8. DAVIS HALL
9. DAI HALL
10. CORY HALL
11. GOLDMAN SCHOOL OF PUBLIC POLICY
12. STANLEY HALL
13. STERN HALL
14. HEARST GREEK THEATRE
15. LEWIS HALL
16. EARL F. CHEIT HALL
17. WOMEN'S FACULTY CLUB
18. SENIOR HALL
19. FACULTY CLUB
20. STEPHENS HALL
21. CAMPANILE
22. SOUTH HALL
23. CAMPUS POWER PLANT
24. ALUMNI HOUSE

WALK #5

CAMPUS WALK
DURATION: **1 hour, 30 minutes**
DISTANCE: **2.6 miles**
STEPS: **613**
DIFFICULTY: **3**
BUS: **7, 52, 65, 67, R, P,**
Downtown Berkeley BART

This is a real snipe-hunt of a walk—a long, twisty, figure-eight trek covering much of the Cal campus. Because there are no intersections or street signs, pay careful attention to the lefts and rights and landmarks.

Begin your walk at the West Gate side of the campus, at the intersection of Addison Street and Oxford Street, after a wiener from Top Dog, a coffee from Starbucks, or a breakfast at The Sunny Side Café, all a block south on Oxford. Then walk directly east from Oxford, toward the campus, up the broad asphalt pathway, to a set of eight wide brick stairs. Take these to a broad plaza featuring a handsome compass rose—a gift to the university from the Class of 1902—and then climb three more steps to the driveway. To the left you'll see Cal's newest building—the Center for Biomedical and Health Sciences.

Cross the driveway to the right and take the sidewalk as it edges past a parking kiosk on the left, and a tall stand of pine and eucalyptus trees on the right. Beneath those trees runs Strawberry Creek, which you'll have ample opportunity to visit as the walk proceeds.

Follow the driveway toward a traffic roundabout centered around a huge old eucalyptus tree. Stay to the right of this and take the asphalt pathway heading up and to the right—using as your landmark the needle-thin Campanile rising before you.

On the right is the stately Life Sciences Building—a 1930 structure, built on the site of the university's old arboretum—with its bas relief carvings of life science figures like the lion, the crab and the ram, and the ancient scientists studying them, all presided over by winged griffons. If you have time, take the 13 steps up to the main building, enter and take seven more, and visit the central atrium, where you will find a fully-preserved, life-sized T-Rex on display, caged in a lovely circular staircase, with a pterodactyl hanging over his head.

If you don't have time for that, walk past the Life Sciences building and bend to the right, passing on its side, and heading for the first set of campus stairs. These you'll find on your left. Rise up 19 wide concrete steps, cross a driveway and circle a flagpole, and climb 12 more to arrive at the door of California Hall, a John Galen Howard building dating from 1905, featuring an oxidized copper roof, in places supporting glass skylight panels.

Turn left at the California Hall doors, walk past the front of the building, and then turn right at the wide sidewalk. Aim uphill, where you'll see your next set of stairs—a set of 31 concrete steps, flanked by shiny steel handrails, in the shade of a low-growing conifer.

Take these to the wide brick plaza fronting the University Library building. Lean on the marble balustrade to admire the sloping lawns and walkways before you, and consider this: Historical photos and drawings show that the land on which the campus sits was a wide sloping plain, entirely flat—until Frederick Law Olmstead, famous for designing New York's Central Park, began landscaping the campus property to give it perspective and character.

Drop down 12 steps heading north, as if you were exiting

the library itself, and walk due north, keeping the lawn on your right. Then, after a short bit, watch for a left turn past Memorial Pool—a quiet, somber spot donated to the university by the classes of 1945–1947, to honor the students and faculty killed during WWII. Just beyond the fountain, take 13 steps down to a paved pathway. Turn right, meet a driveway, and turn right again.

Climb a slight rise. On your left is an impressive modern building with a red-tile roof. This is the C.V. Starr East Asian Library. When you meet its steps, on the left, take them—16 steps up to the library level, past the front doors, and up a final 28 steps straight ahead. Note as you climb the peculiar funnel-like design: The walls slope out, and the staircase becomes narrower as it nears the top.

Make a hairpin right turn when you arrive at the top, and head back down the driveway, with the tall Campanile ahead and to your left. Then, halfway down this slight slope, turn left into a plaza that features a crude saber-tooth tiger statue—shiny where he's been rubbed for good luck. (The *Smilodon californicus* statue's artist was, in a bizarre footnote, the famed Trader Vic's restaurateur Victor Bergeron. Vic was a lifelong friend and apprentice to the San Francisco sculptor Beniamino Bufano, and his bronze statues often used native California animals for their inspiration.) Past the statue, on your left, between McCone and McLaughlin Halls, climb three short steps to a lovely spiral staircase of 33 winding risers.

These will deposit you in a strange industrial space, a bleak landscape of gravel and cooling towers. Walk past this to find a set of 11 stairs dropping straight ahead, and then a set of 24 stairs on the right. Climb up, and emerge before a pair of lounging bronze bears. Turn slightly left, cross the lawn and the driveway, and face the front of Davis Hall.

You'll see a staircase directly across from you. Climb these, up 21 and then 15 steps, to the side of Davis Hall. If you have time, turn left and enter the building at the first door. Inside is a massive engineering playground. Behind glass screens, one floor down, is an array of giant equipment doing experiments, on a huge scale, in applied force and pressure. To the left is the recently-completed Dai Hall. It has a café inside that serves Peet's coffee—a percolating campus perk.

After those delights, turn right. Walk south, keeping the Campanile ahead and to your right, past a set of low brown wooden structures that sometimes function as a café. Turn left past these, and walk along a pleasantly landscaped garden area that features, on the right side, charming covered study stations. At the garden's end, turn left. Climb six steps onto a sidewalk leading beneath an imposing glass catwalk, several stories up. Directly ahead, step up a handsome wide staircase of 34 risers decorated with polished steel handrails.

You arrive on Hearst Avenue. Take a right, and begin walking uphill. On your right is Cory Hall. Across the street at 2607 is a beautifully-maintained timber frame building, designed by Ernest Coxhead, that was the home of fraternity Beta Theta Pi from 1893 to 1966, and now houses the Goldman School of Public Policy.

Turn right onto a narrow path just before Hearst meets La Loma. Pass beneath some stately eucalyptus trees. Watch for a staircase on your right, and drop down 66 stairs, again with a view of the Campanile.

Walk straight ahead. On the first floor of the next building is Yali's, a good place to stop for a coffee or a facilities visit. If you don't need either of those, turn left, and head slightly uphill, onto a series of staircases interrupted by brick walkways and flanked by lovely Japanese maples. Climb a total of 62 stairs to land on Gayley Avenue. Turn right, and walk along the sidewalk.

To your right is Stanley Hall. Up and to your left is Stern Hall, part of the compound of women's dormitories. Go straight ahead, using the crosswalk to cross the street where Gayley comes to an intersection with University Drive. Just ahead, just past the bus stop, you'll find a narrow set of redwood stairs dropping off to the right. Take these 27 steps down and turn left. Skirt a narrow bowling-alley of a lawn, along the back of Lewis Hall. You'll see a set of stairs going back up to Gayley, on your left. Ignore these, but look to the right and find a set of stairs going down—32 steps, with a steel railing.

Walk straight ahead, toward a stand of shaggy Sequoia redwoods, taking the drive and keeping the redwoods on your right. Just ahead of you on the left will be Earl F. Cheit Hall, part of the Haas School of Business. But before you get there, look for a break in the hedge on your right and a walkway. Take this paved path and 11 steps down to the front door of the old Women's Faculty Club. This charming building is another John Galen Howard design from 1923. It now functions, among other things, as a hotel for visiting faculty, parents, and tourists.

Walk straight ahead, taking two more steps up and following the path as it curves along the back side of one of the campus' strangest structures—a real live log cabin, anchored on its corners by massive redwoods. This is Senior Hall, once known as Senior Men's Hall, built in 1906 under the supervision of John Galen Howard, and paid for by a "secret society" called The Order of the Golden Bear. Members of the society still maintain the structure, and meet there regularly—in secrecy.

Just past the log cabin, the path will come to a "T." Turn right, and cross Strawberry Creek on a wooden footbridge. Then turn left and cross the creek again, over a second footbridge, this one running past a tiny waterfall. On your left is another faculty club—originally the men's faculty club and, like its distaff equivalent, is now an on-campus hotel. It was built in 1903 from designs by Bernard Maybeck.

Keep that building on your left, and walk past its broad lawns until the path turns right. Cross Strawberry Creek once more, this time on a strange concrete stair-bridge—a gift to the university by Phoebe Hearst, the newspaper magnate William Randolph Hearst's mother—that rises 26 steps, under a massive and somewhat pointless arch, to deliver you with great ceremony onto a nondescript piece of driveway. (Little-known Cal factoid: The design plan for the original Cal campus was decided by an invitation-only architecture competition held in 1898, and paid for by Phoebe Hearst. A Frenchman named Emile Benard won the competition, but declined to oversee the construction. That job went to John Galen Howard.)

Turn left down this driveway, then turn left at your first opportunity, dropping down a sloping sidewalk and crossing Strawberry Creek once again. Dead ahead you will see the bronze statue honoring Lynn O. "Pops" Waldorf, the colorful Cal football coach from 1947–1957. Before you go that far, turn right and walk between two decorative stone lanterns, across a wide bridge that leads into the back of Stephens Hall. Take the brick staircase on your right and climb up 41 steps and over several landings that lead up and through the hall itself.

You emerge before the majestic Campanile. Walk straight ahead. Climb 10 steps to the obelisk's base, where a bust of Abraham Lincoln presides mournfully. Circle the base of the Campanile, if you like. On the opposite side is a memorial to its creator, the architect John Galen Howard, who was the principal architect of the campus, and who designed many of its signature buildings—the Greek Theater, the Sather Gate, and Sather Tower, better known as the Campanile. If it is a weekday between 10:00 a.m. and 3:45 p.m., or a weekend day between 10:00 a.m. and 4:45 p.m. (except for Sunday between 1:30 and 3:30 p.m.) you can go inside and take an elevator ride to the top of the tower. It's free for students, $2 for everyone else, and well worth the ride. As you visit, consider this odd fact: several floors of the Campanile house dinosaur bones and fossils, excavated in the early 1900s by a Cal professor from the famous La Brea Tar Pits of Los Angeles. These are not open to the public, but it's nice to know they're there, isn't it?

Find your way to the western or downhill side of the Campanile, where late afternoon views often feature a beautiful sunset and a vista that includes the Golden Gate Bridge. Drop down 21 steps, cross the wide driveway, and descend five steps more. On your left is South Hall, one of the oldest structures on campus. Dating from 1873, South Hall used to have a twin, North Hall, standing where the Bancroft Library now stands. The legend that scenes from Mary Poppins were filmed on the South

Hall rooftop is, apparently, only legend.

Turn left and walk behind this fine old building. Beyond it, drop down 26 bricked stairs and across a wooden bridge. On your right, framed by heavy oak trees, is the campus power plant. This sturdy brick building, a 1904 John Galen Howard design, was originally the campus art gallery. That's why the walls facing you are decorated with delightful mosaic murals featuring painters, sculptors, and musicians at work.

Turn right, past the power plant building, and walk through a parking lot and into a vast, wide plaza. To your right is Howard's famed Sather Gate. (Like the Campanile, it is named in honor of Peder Sather, a Norwegian-born banker who made his fortune in the Bay Area, and who was one of the trustees of the College of California, which became UC Berkeley. After his death, his widow donated the money to erect the gate and the tower in his name.) To your left is the Golden Bear Café. Aim straight ahead, between these two structures, descending slightly along a line of aged sequoia redwoods.

Keep the creek on your right. Pass a bridge. Across the gully, you'll see a set of redwood shingled Craftsman buildings. On your left is a handsome Asian-themed Alumni House—elements of which were part of a gift to Cal from the Alumni Association of Japan in 1934. Note the stone temple lamp in the garden.

Just before the pathway meets a parking lot—across which you can see the back of the original Cal football stadium, now used principally for track and field events—turn right and cross the creek once again, this time on a wide wooden footbridge. Cross the roadway ahead of you in the crosswalk, and bear left along the pathway, keeping the creek on your left. Follow the path as it crosses the creek again, and then turns and crosses a final time—over a bridge whose railing is decorated with twin Stars of David.

Follow the creek down. In time you will arrive at the corner of Oxford and Center Street. Turn right and walk a block to Addison, and you will be back at your starting point.

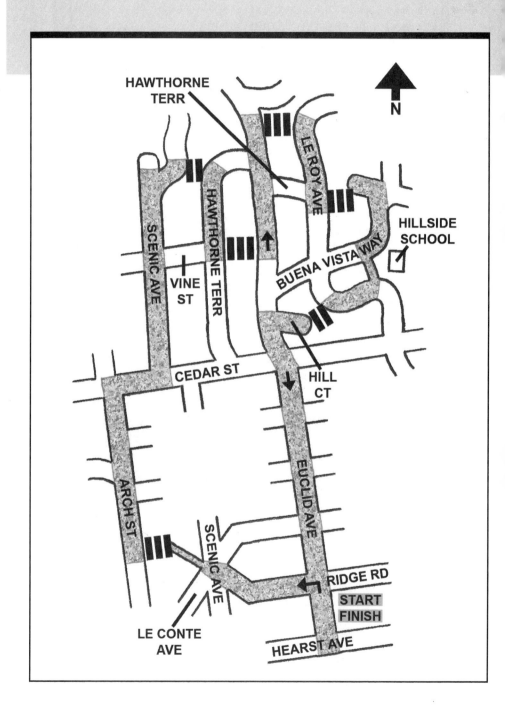

WALK #6

HOLY HILL
DURATION: **1 hour, 30 minutes**
DISTANCE: **2.6 miles**
STEPS: **244**
DIFFICULTY: **3**
BUS: **65, 52**

This is a delightful stroll, lined with houses from some of Berkeley's most celebrated architects and dotted with some of Berkeley's most charming staircases, interrupted by pleasant stretches of easy, flat walking.

Begin your walk at the northern end of the campus, near the corner of Euclid and Hearst Avenues, perhaps with a snack from one of the many eateries on this block, or a good strong coffee from Nefeli Caffe at 1854 Euclid. When you're ready, walk north on Euclid, uphill, with the campus at your back.

Euclid used to be home to an important streetcar line, inaugurated in 1903, that served residents of this very steep hillside community. Many of the original staircases were designed specifically to deliver streetcar passengers to and from the line. It was also home to so many religious institutions that the slope you're on right now—formerly known as Wilson's Hill—became known as "Holy Hill." Turn left at the first corner, onto Ridge Road, to find out why.

On the right is the first of several buildings belonging to the Church Divinity School of the Pacific, an Episcopal seminary and theological center, founded in San Mateo in 1893, that has made Ridge Road its home since 1930. (Next door is the Geochronology Institution, a scientific study organization dedicated to determining the exact age of the Earth, among other things.) On the left, perched on Holy Hill but not affiliated to it, are the student co-ops Casa Zimbabwe and Ridge House, the latter a 1906 half-timbered Arts and Crafts design from John Galen Howard, who was the master architect of the Berkeley campus, and the designer responsible for signature Cal buildings like its Campanile, its Greek Theater, and its Sather Gate. The more modern building just after this, on the left, is the Graduate Theological Union Library, by post-modern designer Louis I. Kahn. On the right, as you near the corner, are the matched set of Gothic-style brick buildings Gibbs Hall and All Saints Chapel. Both are part of the Church Divinity School of the Pacific's Holy Hill campus, and both were built by Walter H. Ratcliff Jr. who, along with Bernard C. Maybeck, was perhaps Berkeley's most prolific architect. The brick building on the corner, not part of the Ratcliff set, is a 1923 design from Stafford L. Jory.

At the corner of the complicated intersection, walk straight ahead, crossing Scenic Avenue and Le Conte Avenue, and walking onto another seminary, this time the Pacific School of Religion—a non-denominational Christian seminary dating from 1866. The entire campus was a Ratcliff design, and his influence is palpable. Especially nice is the moody, Gothic Holbrook Building and the Charles Holbrook Library, built in 1925 but feeling much older.

Follow the walkway straight ahead until you can walk no more, then find your first staircase. Descend 35 steps, down and to the right, off the seminary campus and onto an elevated walkway. Follow the walkway downhill onto Arch Street. Walk along, past Virginia Street and Hilgard Avenue, through a neighborhood that once boasted many historic houses. The terrible fires of 1923, however, destroyed most of them, and most were replaced by the apartment buildings you see here now.

Turn right onto Cedar Street, then turn left where you meet Scenic Avenue again. As you cross, you may see some Roman numerals carved into the top of the curb. You may see these all over the East Bay. I was mystified by them—ancient runes? hiking hieroglyphics?—until a street maintenance worker explained that these markings indicate the location of important water and power features in the middle of the street, so people won't dig into them or pave over them. A sign reading "XI" here, next to an arrow, means there is a manhole cover or access point for water or gas, 11 feet thataway.

Scenic gradually rises, and the homes and views increase in stature. Cross Vine Street and continue uphill, watching for a contractor's stamp in the sidewalk (poured in 1908) on the right side of the road and the fine shingled houses at 1452 and 1446. Then bear right as the street bears right, and look on your right side for the bottom of Hawthorne Steps.

This one begins with 15 steps onto a sloping sidewalk and is fitted with handrails. Cross beneath a sweeping African tree fern, and climb 37 more steps to land on Hawthorne Terrace. Turn right and walk downhill, admiring the fine redwoods and the fine views.

Admire also the homes, for this is a line of signature buildings from Berkeley's most venerated architects. Directly before you on the corner lot is a 1924 home from John Hudson Thomas, who, like John Galen Howard and Bernard Maybeck (he studied under both men at Cal), was a prized local architect. Next door is another Thomas from the same year. Next door to that, heading downhill on the left side of the street, is a collection of massive stucco-and-beam homes by Henry Higby Gutterson, all from 1924–1925. (Gutterson was another Howard student, and a graduate of Cal's first architecture class in 1906. He went on to work for Howard's firm, before starting his own design company in 1914.) The huge structure on the right, at 1440 and 1450, is actually *two* homes, a Gutterson matched set built for a brother and sister to share, with a shared garden in between. Many of these, you'll note, share an unusual roof

An old redwood, survivor of the Berkeley hills fires.

tile design, a salmon-colored riff on the classic Mexican tile half-circle.

At the next intersection, where Vine Street comes in on the right, find quaint Vine Lane on the left. This walkway begins under a low-hanging oak tree and rises 43 steps, with a double handrail, under deep shade, to land on Euclid Avenue once more. It would appear this is a true walk-street, and that some of the houses, the delightful cottage at 3 Vine Lane in particular, have no other street access but the walkway.

Turn left onto Euclid, pausing to admire the charming "Vine Lane" sign above you. Admire, too, the vast English Tudor across the street. Said to be the largest house in this entire region, it is a Walter Ratcliff Jr. construction from 1929. Note in particular the gigantic window onto the garden—perhaps not original to the house.

When you're done admiring all that, walk uphill on Euclid. Pass a turn for Hawthorne Terrace on the right, and another on the left. Continue to the crosswalk, and look across the street to admire Rose Walk.

This is generally admired as Berkeley's most beautiful walk-street. You can see why. The approach is up an elegant double-sided staircase, fronted by a stone bench, and was designed by Bernard C. Maybeck. The modest but handsome small homes lining the walk were all designed by Henry Gutterson, and all built between 1924–1928.

Cross Euclid and climb the 22 steps up onto Rose Walk, and stroll past the sweet cottages and well-tended gardens, and under the stately period lamp posts. The sidewalk drifts up into heavy redwood shade, and leads to another staircase, which rises 17 steps to a sidewalk. Turn right, and walk south along Le Roy Avenue.

The house immediately to your right, at 1400, is a Julia Morgan home from 1910, rebuilt after the fires in 1923, when its second story was destroyed. Across the street, note the peculiar tower rising from the garage. My guess: It's an elevator shaft, to get people and groceries from the car to the house.

Head downhill on Le Roy. Where Hawthorne Terrace comes in again on the right, look left, find the bottom of the beautiful La Loma Steps, and begin to climb. The house to the immediate left is a 1925 John Hudson Thomas. To the immediate right is another—same architect, same year. In the middle, built in 1910 and rebuilt in 1992, is a rose-colored gallery and brick walkway. It begins under an ivy-covered arbor, walks up 21 steps onto a brick path, and turns through a pink overhang of wood and vine. The brick pathway climbs some more and rises 24 steps to finish under another arbor on Buena Vista Avenue.

Stop to notice the house across the street: The rose-colored theme appears to have spread onto this William Garren home from 1927. Turn right, and head downhill on Buena Vista, where in fact the vistas are not yet so *buena*. (That will come, shortly.) As you descend, notice another Ratcliff at 2583, a Maybeck at 2577, and another Garren at 2573. This last one is ornamented by a curious image of a three-legged woman, a symbol similar to the one you will find on the menus at the College Avenue Italian restaurant Trattoria La Siciliana. Hmm.

Continue down the hill. Where Buena Vista bends right, turn left, across the crosswalk, and enter the grounds of the historic Hillside School. Walk straight ahead, across the front of the building, which is a delightful Walter Ratcliff Jr. construction from 1925. It was once a public school, but now houses a smattering of smaller concerns, among them the Berkeley Chess Club.

When you reach the street on the other side of the school, turn right onto another stretch of Le Roy. Walk along a short block, with the school playground on your right. Where the street bends right, look left, just after the white adobe house at 1544, and find the narrow entrance to Hill Court Steps.

This starts as a tight walkway, passing closely between the houses, that then turns left and drops down four steps to another walkway. Stop here and get the *buena vista* you may have missed before—a staggering view on a clear day of all Oakland, the Bay Bridge, the Golden Gate Bridge, and all points in between. Then drop down 20 more steps, bending right, to drop onto the cul-de-sac end of tiny Hill Court. Walk to the end of the block, and turn left again onto Euclid.

Stay on the left side of the street, and drop down six steps to cross Cedar. Staying on Euclid, cross Hilgard once more and then Virginia. You return now to Holy Hill, or the flatlands around it. On your left, behind the metal gates at 1727, is Yun Lin Temple Cultural Center, with its brightly-painted walkway contrasting the serene Krishna meditating in the front yard. It was once the Del Ray Club, designed by the firm Masten & Hurd in 1924. Then on the right is the Franciscan School of Theology, originally the Tau Kappa Epsilon fraternity house, also a Masten & Hurd from 1924.

Across Le Conte is the backside of the Church School of the Pacific's Geochronology Institute. Straight ahead, Euclid crosses Ridge and descends toward Hearst—and returns you to your starting point.

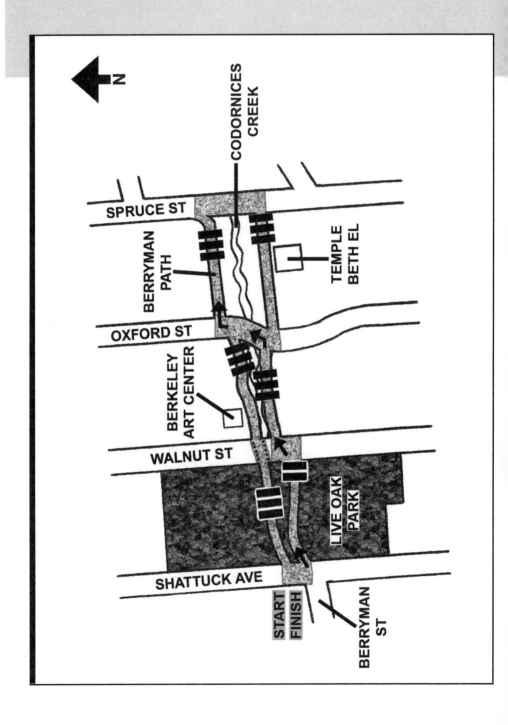

WALK #7

BERRYMAN STATION
DURATION: **30 minutes**
DISTANCE: **0.8 miles**
STEPS: **89**
DIFFICULTY: **1.5**
BUS: **18, 7, 67**

This very gentle walk hardly qualifies as a stair walk at all, but it's centered around one of Berkeley's most charming small parks and features some interesting historic elements. It's a fine choice for a lunch-hour or picnic stroll.

Begin this short walk at the western side of Live Oak Park, near the intersection of Shattuck Avenue and Berryman Street. Enter Live Oak Park, just to the right of the weathered sign bearing the park's name. Walk straight ahead, 25 feet or so on the rose-colored pavement, with the park building on your right, then veer left down toward the bridge. Cross the bridge, and bear right to walk along the creek and picnic area. On the other side of this, take 12 steps on the right to climb up to street level. Cross Walnut Street, turn left, and at the wide sidewalk, bordered by a steel handrail, enter the top half of the park.

Directly to your left is the Berkeley Art Center, open to the public Wednesday through Sunday, 12:00 to 5:00 p.m. For now, walk past this, sloping down past a fire pit and rustic amphitheater on your right, heading for the set of wooden steps rising up ahead of you. Take these and climb 20 steps to a ramp with green handrails that winds up and around, and ends at Oxford Street.

Turn left onto Oxford, walk over a bridge that crosses the creek below, and then cross the street using the crosswalk. Walk straight ahead, and up one step, to an asphalt path running up through the trees. This is Berryman Path, as it extends above Live Oak Park. It wanders through the trees, as a narrow, leafy lane in the shade, to emerge, up nine final steps, onto Spruce Street.

Turn right. Walk past the first driveway, turn right, and walk down seven broad steps. Continue onto the driveway running through the Temple Beth El property. When you return to Oxford Street, stop and look to the right. You'll find an informational plaque telling the tale of the Napoleon Byrne House, a dynamic Italianate mansion, built in 1868, which once stood at this location.

"Nappy" Byrne was an intriguing fellow. Arriving from Missouri by covered wagon, traveling with a large family and two freed slaves—said to have been Berkeley's first African American residents—he acquired a huge tract of land abutting Codornices Creek, and set to raising stock. He built an immense home, had financial reversals, and failed. The house was sold to Henry Berryman, who used it as the base of an empire that, at one time, included a water company, a railway, and a subdivision of homes. The rail line ran up Shattuck to within a block of where Live Oak Park stands today.

Cross Oxford and turn right, taking note of the humorous M. C. Escher-style geese on the house at 1282. Then cross the bridge over Codornices Creek once more, but this time turn left where the crosswalk hits the street, and find a staircase dropping 24 steps down to the creek level. Follow the path as it follows the creek, aiming for the Berkeley Art Center. Veer left around the building, onto a wooden porch, then turn left onto the wide wooden entrance, lined with headless telephone poles. Where the wood meets the asphalt path, bear right, and follow the asphalt down and into the tunnel crossing beneath Walnut.

Admire the artistic tagging here, and emerge on the other side. Walk toward a little bridge, cross this, and hang a right back toward the immense stone chimney that seems to stand alone in the trees. This is the remnant of a 1915 residence that was later destroyed by fire. Note the heavy metal doors, and the ashes within: It's still a working fireplace.

Walk past the fireplace and catch the 16 steps up to a ramp leading to the park's north side. Here you will find wide walkways circling wide lawns. Head down and left, and aim for a very narrow wooden pedestrian bridge. This will carry you over the creek once more, past a stone marking the tercentenary of Finnish-American presence in Berkeley, placed by "K. N. Tammettaren Tupan No. 35" in 1938. Helpful information.

Just after this you emerge from shade onto Shattuck, beside Berryman. This is the beginning of this walk, and the end.

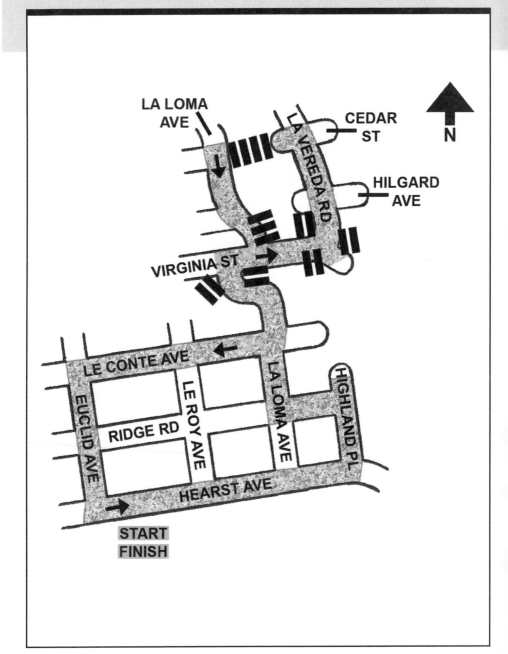

WALK #8

NORTHSIDE
DURATION: **1 hour, 15 minutes**
DISTANCE: **2 miles**
STEPS: **238**
DIFFICULTY: **2**
BUS: **65**

This gentle walk is relatively free of stairs, but packed with architecture and design. Many of the old homes survived the devastating 1923 Berkeley fire; several others survived the spreading of the Cal campus, which replaced some historic homes with university buildings like Etcheverry Hall, Soda Hall, and an unsightly parking structure. The surviving homes represent the work of the area's most important early architects.

Start your stroll near the Northgate entrance to the campus, at the corner of Hearst and Euclid Avenues, perhaps with a fine coffee from Nefeli or a snack at one of the many campus-adjacent eateries. When you are sated, begin walking east on Hearst, heading uphill from Euclid.

The big apartment building on the corner to your left is the work of John Galen Howard, a local designer who was supervising architect for the Cal campus master plan and who designed many of its iconic structures, among them the famed Campanile, the Greek Theater, and Sather Gate. The structure is now the Euclid Apartments, and features a peculiar clam shell motif near its roofline that is similar to the roadside markings for the pilgrims' way to Spain's Santiago de Compostela. Galen was also responsible for the two imposing shingle-sided buildings on your right, which are part of the Cal architecture department—which he himself founded in 1894. All three buildings were constructed between 1912–1913. Across the road are the newer Etcheverry and Soda Hall buildings. Will anyone care, in the future, who designed *them?*

At the corner of Le Roy Avenue, note the charming "medieval village," an 1893 design from architect Ernest Coxhead, home to Beta Theta Pi, and said to be the oldest fraternity house in the north campus area.

Continue up Hearst, then turn left onto Highland Place. Rising on your right is the Nyingma Institute, where devotees study a centuries old form of Tibetan Buddhism. The building, originally the Psi Upsilon Chapter House, was constructed in 1912 by Benjamin McDougall, who also did downtown Berkeley's famous Shattuck Hotel. Continue on up Highland, crossing Ridge Road, and look to the left. Hidden in the trees are the Charles Keeler house and studio—the earliest known commissions of Berkeley architect Bernard Maybeck. This designer was a transplanted New Yorker who had studied at the Ecole des Beaux Arts in Paris, and later became a professor of engineering drawing at Cal. He built these two cottages between 1895 and 1902, and would later design the famous Palace of Fine Arts building in San Francisco and the remarkable First Church of Christ, Scientist at 2619 Dwight Way, in Berkeley.

Return to Ridge, turn right, and walk downhill. As you go, admire the fine liquidambar trees that line the sidewalk, then turn right onto La Loma Avenue. On your right, note the sturdy clinker-brick wall and chimney of the Fannie Bitting house, a 1902 "simple home" construction from F. E. Armstrong.

At the next corner, where La Loma meets Le Conte, cross the street and head slightly uphill, following La Loma as it continues to rise. Staying on the right side, find and climb the 13 steps at 1715 La Loma to the uphill side of the street, and the sidewalk. Across and behind you is a large stucco home designed by Julia Morgan and Ira Hoover. Directly up the hill, on your right, are two fine examples from Bernard Maybeck: The

1911 Jockers house at 1709, and the magnificent chalet-style Rees house on the corner at 1705.

Climb six steps onto Virginia Street and turn right, following the Rees property line up the hill. At the end of the block, on the right side, you will find the La Vereda Steps. This is an elegant structure connecting Virginia Street to La Vereda Road. It rises 24 steps, past a landing that offers fine views of the bay, to land near the very good-looking Pope-Bray house, a 1911 design from Carl Ericsson.

Head left up the roadway, then take the second part of the La Vereda Steps up to your right. These rise nine steps to a "T" intersection. Turn right, and continue up 13 wide wooden steps, across a driveway with a wooden bridge, and on to another 23 steps up to the high end of the road. Note the fine big Dutch farmhouse at 1730, an 1896 design by Frank May.

Above you, the steps continue in wood up the hillside. This is part of a path that rises to the Lawrence Berkeley National Laboratory high above. They are not for you. Instead, cross the street and find another set of stairs, 12 this time, dropping down onto the sidewalk in front of the bungalows at 1731–35.

Then, because this *is* a stairs book, cross the pavement beside the manhole at the top of the La Vereda Steps structure, and drop down 23 steps to the lower part of the road. Turn right, and walk onto La Vereda Road.

Behind you, notice a sign that reads "Very Small Cars Only." Ahead, to your right, notice a fine wide porch at 1631, on an 1895 house designed by local architect George Jensen. At the corner, cross Hilgard, past a sleek-sided box of a house at 1615. Then, at the next corner, turn left into the "Not A Through Street" end of Cedar Street. This looks an awful lot like a private driveway, but…at the bottom, on the right, next to the garage for the house at 2710, is the top of Cedar Path.

Descend this narrow trail, beneath oaky shade, 66 redwood tie steps down, bearing left as the trail nears the street below, and down a final 11 steps to land on the sidewalk. You're on La Loma, once again. Walk straight ahead on the sidewalk, heading downhill. Stay to the left side of the street, and notice a plaque to the aforementioned George Jensen, at 1675. This home, which was the Jensen family residence, was one of only 50 in the area not destroyed in the 1923 Berkeley fire—in part because the property had its own water well.

Continue on to the next corner. Take four steps down from sidewalk to street. Then make a straight line to the middle of the intersection, and take 15 steps down to the downhill side of the street. Bear left, staying on La Loma as it crosses Virginia, and take 19 more steps down to the lowest section of La Loma. Continue downhill in the deep shade here.

Turn right where La Loma meets Le Conte again. You'll get a sideways look at a John Hudson Thomas Arts and Crafts duplex on the right, at 2667–69. The turret is apparently not original, but was added in the 1970s when the building housed an ashram.

At Le Roy, turn left to admire the strange Weltevreden half-hidden in the trees at 1775. It is marked as Tellefsen Hall and now houses the Cal university band, but it was once said to be the most famous residence in all Berkeley. Designer A. C. Schweinfurth, like Julia Morgan, a favorite of William Randolph Hearst, built the clinker-brick mansion in 1896 for a prominent banker named Volney Moody. It became a fraternity house in the 1920s. Schweinfurth also designed the Unitarian Church on the other side of campus, on Bancroft Avenue.

Return to Le Conte and turn left. Turn left again onto Euclid, and walk the last downhill bit to Hearst, where you will find your starting point.

OVERLEAF: A BERKELEY VIEW OF THE BAY AND BRIDGE.

PART TWO

BERKELEY:
THE NORTH

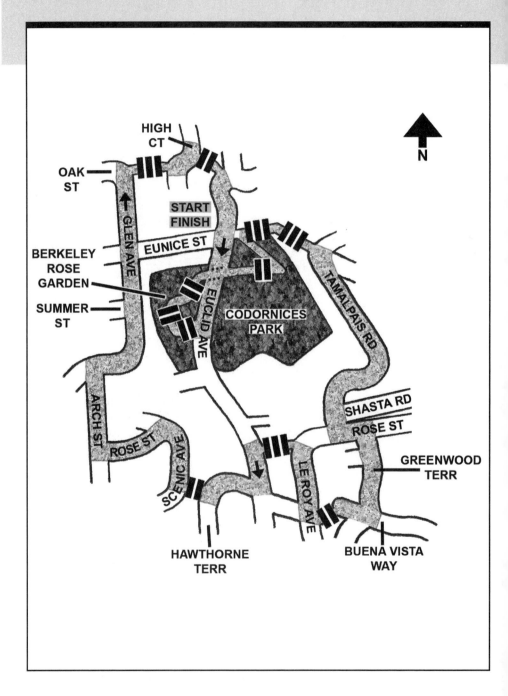

WALK #9

"ROSE" WALK
DURATION: **1 hour, 30 minutes**
DISTANCE: **1.6 miles**
STEPS: **554**
DIFFICULTY: **3.5**
BUS: **65**

This rose-themed walk is short and energetic, with a steep climb into one of Berkeley's most charming neighborhoods, and includes a short tour of the famed Berkeley Rose Garden.

Begin this walk on Euclid Avenue and Eunice Street, near Codornices Park. With the hills behind you, walk south to the wide semi-circle entrance of the Berkeley Rose Garden. Find the steps to your left, and begin.

Take 10 steps down to a path, then 16 steps down to a gate, then veer left and take seven steps down onto another path. Walk across a short wooden bridge, then up two steps, and follow the path down to the right. Then take 50 wooden steps down a series of switchbacks to land at the very bottom of the Rose Garden property. Take the path straight ahead of you, across the bottom of the garden.

This is a fine piece of civic beauty, containing over 3,000 rose bushes, in 250 different varieties. It is a point of pride amongst locals that no pesticides are used in the growing of these roses. The tall fencing is designed to protect the roses from those other locals, the rosebud-nibbling deer.

The garden was built during the Depression as a Works Progress Administration project, between 1933 and 1937. Its 220-foot-long redwood pergola was designed by Bernard Maybeck. The best rose-viewing period is said to be mid-May.

Even if it's not mid-May, continue across the bottom of the garden to another wooden bridge. Take four steps up, then find the concrete steps with metal handrails to your left—38 wide steps up to the top. The tennis courts will be straight ahead of you. Bear right, and walk under Maybeck's wooden arbor, flanked with rose bushes. Fans of "letterboxing" may find a letterbox somewhere in this garden. For everyone else, walk past the drinking fountain and turn left, up three stairs toward a gate out of the garden.

Head left, walking with the tennis courts on your left and, after a bit, a wooden public facilities building on your right. Then, just past that, turn right and walk through the pedestrian tunnel passing under Euclid, delivering you to Codornices Park. This is one of Berkeley's oldest city parks, dating from 1915. Its original design included tennis courts and a field house.

Walk straight ahead, across the playground, aiming for a set of steps, next to a popular concrete slide, under a majestic spreading oak tree. Climb these 41 steps—mindful of the low branches—to the top of the slide. Turn left and drift downhill on the pathway, keeping the wooden handrail on your left.

Stay on the trail, ignoring the stairs on your left, until you come to a flat place with wooden bridges to the left and to the right—one public, one private—both of them crossing Codornices Creek. To the far right, find the curving concrete staircase. This is Tamalpais Path, one of Berkeley's finest public staircases. It rises a total of 183 steps, over many landings, under a canopy of magnificent redwood trees, and through a charming canyon unfortunately decorated by graffiti on a bordering fence.

To your left, a path and gate lead to one of Berkeley's loveliest spots—a little waterfall section of Codornices Creek. This is private property, but I'm told the owner is happy to have visitors take a peek. Go politely, and tread lightly.

Continuing up, the stairs end beside 149 Tamalpais Road, a 1909 house sometimes described as Berkeley's most romantic private residence. It has a storybook charm, heavenly views, and is handsomely framed in big redwood trees.

Leave that, and walk downhill on Tamalpais. The road drops and begins to level, passing substantial redwood shingle homes (I admired 85, 77, and 31), then begins to curve and rise again. It crosses the lowest portion of Shasta Road, then meets the uppermost portion of Rose Street. Turn left onto Rose, careful of cars spinning up Tamalpais, and walk up one short block.

Dead ahead is Rose Steps, a concrete structure that goes from shady, silent Rose Street onto busy La Loma Avenue. It's a great shortcut, but not a very attractive staircase. So don't go there. Instead, turn right onto Greenwood Terrace.

This flat street features some lovely homes with lovely views. But it also features Greenwood Commons, which, despite its name, is a private residential block halfway down the terrace. Signs on the driveway ask walkers not to bring their dogs with them, which suggests the residents don't want walkers to stay out entirely. So walk on—but be on your best walking behavior. Greenwood Commons was conceived by William Wurstler, then dean of Cal's College of Environmental Design, with gardens designed by Lawrence Halprin. Eight houses share the common green space, fronting houses designed by mid-century architects—among them Donald Olsen, Harwell Hamilton Harris, John Funk, and others.

Follow the driveway to a path off to the left, which circles around and stops, and presents you with a view as nice as any residential view in the Berkeley hills. Pause, admire, then move on.

Return to Greenwood Terrace, turn right, and walk until the road falls and meets Buena Vista Way. Turn right, drop down 100 feet or so and, just after the house at 2595, find your next staircase. This one begins under an arbor supported by faded rose-colored columns, which in color and texture exactly match the house across the street, directly behind you. Drop 45 steps down into a deeply shaded bower, concluding beneath another rose-colored overhang, this one festooned with wisteria.

This is the La Loma Steps, curiously named because they do not connect with La Loma Avenue. They will have delivered you to Le Roy Avenue, between the houses at 1497 and 1501. There are houses with pedigree all around—1497 is a John Hudson Thomas from 1925, as is 1464; the two Mediterraneans at 1454 and 1430 are from Walter Steilberg and the design firm of Sidney and Noble Newsom, also from the mid-1920s.

Cross Le Roy and take a right, heading up a slight incline. There are striking homes here, especially the even-numbered ones on the left side of the street. Just after the large brown structure at 1400—a Julia Morgan home from 1910—you will find another set of stairs, this one marked again by a rose-colored column at the top. Turn left and descend Rose Walk, beginning with 17 steps down, under redwood shade, into a tiny community of old bungalows.

Is there a more attractive walk-street in all of Berkeley? This delightful island of scenic beauty was originally designed by Bernard Maybeck, with homes designed by Henry Higby Gutterson. The units here were often leased to university professors. In time, the property was deeded to the university. In late 2010 the property went on the market. Its nine units—four duplexes and one cottage—had an asking price of $3.4 million.

The wide pathway is bordered by well-tended rose bushes. Walk along this handsome path, then drop down a final 23 steps, going either right or left on this double-barreled staircase, to land on Euclid Avenue.

Cross the street using the crosswalk, then take a backward glance at the Maybeck-designed base of Rose Walk, with its charming trolley benches. Then head south (downhill) on Euclid. After half a block, turn right onto Hawthorne Terrace. The big shingled house at 1404 on your right, as you turn, is a Julia Morgan from 1911. The stucco house at 1411, across the street, is also a Julia Morgan, but from 1926.

A couple of houses in, on your right, watch for tiny Hawthorne Steps. Drop down this shady staircase, 52 steps in all, with a handrail and sloping sidewalk along the way. Where you land, turn right onto Scenic Avenue. Climb up a bit, winding right as the street curves around, then turn left onto Rose Street. Descend, then turn right onto Arch Street.

Across the street and to the left is a fine old home on the corner, a wide-porched beauty, built in 1905 by architect John White. Heading uphill are houses of a similar vintage, including those at 1335 and 1326, from 1907, and those at 1324 and 1320, from the same period (both by Julia Morgan). The houses closest to the corner are even older: 1300 was built in 1905, and 1308 in 1904. The house at 1325 was designed by Bernard Maybeck for the Kroeber family. Mr. Kroeber was Alfred, a Cal professor of anthropology; Mrs. Kroeber was Theodora, author of the acclaimed anthropological study *Ishi in Two Worlds*. Their daughter was Ursula K. Le Guin, the author of popular sci-fi and fantasy novels.

At the corner, turn right onto Glen Avenue. Follow this along as it curves around to the left, and passes Summer Street and Eunice Street. After one more block, where Glen Avenue makes a hard left and turns into Oak Street, look to the right. You're at the end of Oak Street Path.

Follow the walkway to a series of concrete and railroad tie steps, 23 in all, to the cul-de-sac end of a roadway. Walk a block's worth of Laurel Street, and then where Laurel bends and turns into High Court, walk straight ahead, as Oak Street Path continues, onto a length of rose-colored sidewalk. Drop down 40 steps, then follow the sidewalk some more as it turns right and emerges onto Euclid Avenue. Turn right. Walk down Euclid to the corner, where you meet Eunice. On your right, dead ahead, is the Rose Garden, and your starting point.

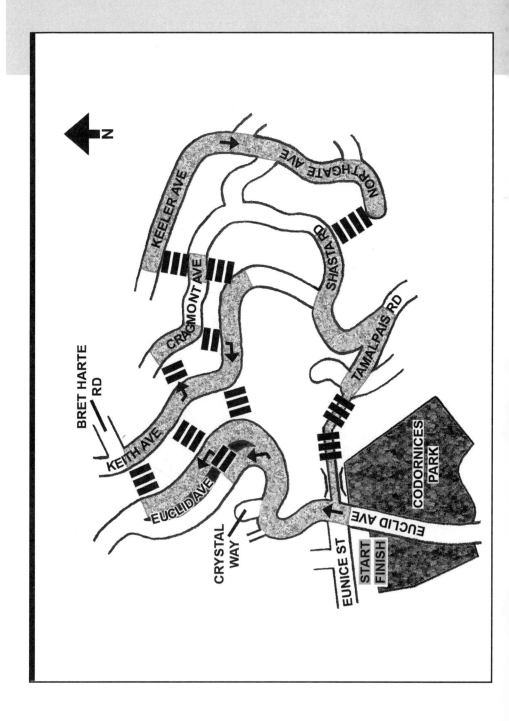

WALK #10

CODORNICES PARK
DURATION: **1 hour, 30 minutes**
DISTANCE: **2.5 miles**
STEPS: **1,230**
DIFFICULTY: **4.5**
BUS: **65**

This is an aggressive hike that ladders up and down the hillside-hanging roads behind Codornices Park. It offers a strenuous workout under heavy redwood shade, and some delightful bay views, and has the highest stair count of any walk in this collection. Because it involves steep hillside sections, it is not recommended during wet or rainy weather.

Begin your walk at the western side of Codornices Park, near the corner of Euclid Avenue and Eunice Street. ("Codornices," for the linguist, means "quails" in Spanish. The creek that gave the park its name was once teeming with them.) With the park on your right, walk north and uphill on Euclid, keeping to the left-hand side of the street.

There are several worthy redwood bungalows on your left, and the turning into charming Oak Street Path. (See "Rose" Walk, Walk #9.) Continue past these, staying on the left side of the street, as Euclid winds around, crosses Crystal Way, and begins to climb. Slow down to enjoy "The Sacred Alignments," a mural "inspired by the Mayan creation story," that decorates the fence on your left. Then, when you reach the house at 1132, cross the divided roadway—*carefully*, watching the downhill traffic— and take the concrete staircase to the uphill, northbound side of

Euclid. Climb 18 steps, cross Euclid, turn left, and walk uphill.

As you walk, reflect on this: A longtime resident remembers that the Euclid street car line was a one-track line, running on the lower half of Euclid. That's why the lower half is wider than the upper.

You might have spied a staircase earlier. You might see another one now. Ignore them, and keep walking. They will come into play later. For the moment, continue up Euclid to just after the house at 1103, and there find the bottom of Bret Harte Way—yet another tribute to the writer who, with his stories *The Luck of Roaring Camp* and *The Outcasts of Poker Flat*, helped Mark Twain give the California Gold Rush much of its color and charm.

This is a steep concrete walkway, fitted with handrails but somewhat uneven, that carries you 42 steps up through a live oak and bamboo bower. You land on Keith Avenue. Turn right, and walk a short distance to the intersection of Keith and the El Mirador Path. You'll come first to a set of stairs going down, on the right. Walk on a bit, and find the uphill section, on your left. This steep set of stairs climbs 135 redwood ties and redwood rounds, to land on Cragmont Avenue next to a house with a conical witch-hat roof.

Turn right. Walk along Cragmont a bit. Just after the house at 1146, find the Martinez Path, going downhill, on your right. Descend sharply, under the shade of thick bamboo, a long 94 steps back down to Keith. Turn right and follow Keith. Just past the house at 1120, turn left and head down El Mirador Path—the bottom half of the part you used earlier to walk up to Cragmont. Now descend a series of concrete steps with rails, somewhat uneven and quite steep, dropping beneath huge redwoods for a total of 74 steps back down to Euclid. Turn left. Head downhill, but don't walk far. Just after the house at 1147, find the Redwood Terrace steps on the left.

At the time of this writing, these stairs were marked with street maintenance cones and were in serious need of help. They're all concrete, and mostly lined with handrails, but they are also terribly uneven, with many broken risers. Go slowly, climbing a total of 134 steps to the top, beneath the welcome shade of big redwood and eucalyptus trees. You land at 1140 Keith.

Across the street is another conical-roofed house, this one a mock-Tudor. Turn right and walk uphill past this house. Note Martinez Path as you go, and enjoy a flat section of wooded roadway lined with big wooden houses. Just past the redwood garages for 1173 and 1175, find the not-so-covert Covert Path on your left.

This is another very steep trail, which starts with a section of 37 redwood switchback steps, then continues along a dirt path into a creeky hollow. Cross the creek, and begin climbing the 116 redwood and concrete steps to the top. Along the way, keep your eyes peeled for wildlife. It's a popular destination for deer.

You land on Cragmont once again. Cross the street and, yes, climb on! Covert Path continues, beginning again in redwood ties and rising sharply up a very steep 164 steps, emerging from deep shade into the sunlight of two unfenced back yards.

You arrive at last at 1146 Keeler. Turn right and walk slightly uphill, enjoying big bay views through the open carports on the right. The architecture is an interestingly mixed bag here. There are unexpected brick structures next door to each other at 1169 and 1173, and a bricky Spanish *hacienda* across the road at 1180.

Ignore Stevenson Path as you pass it—it's part of Remillard Park, Walk #18—as Keeler begins to descend. You'll pass a turning for Shasta Road to the left, and another to the right. Disregard both of these, but continue straight on, as Keeler ends and Northgate Avenue begins. This rises and climbs to the left. As the road flattens, and meets Quail Avenue, bear right, staying on Northgate. At its cul-de-sac culmination, stop and seek out the massive views between the houses. Then, look for the top of Northgate Path amidst a riot of morning glory vines over to your right.

This is a fine piece of staircase engineering that begins in a gentle redwood tie descent of 38 steps and then falls very sharply down a dramatic set of 195 steep redwood steps to end in a well-designed set of switchbacks.

One of the newest staircases in this collection, the Northgate Path was completed in the fall of 2010 by volunteers from the Berkeley Path Wanderers Association. It is a tribute to their hard work, ingenuity, and dedication.

You land at 2573 Shasta Road. Turn left and head downhill as Shasta bends and curves. Walk past the turning for Keith, bearing left as Shasta continues down. Then, where Shasta meets Tamalpais Road, make a hard dog-leg turn to the right beside the big pink house with the little koi pond on the corner.

You find interesting architecture as you descend. The big redwood home at 170 is the Louise Rigg house, a 1979 exercise in bare wood. The Mediterranean at 160, with the olive trees in the front yard, is the 1928 work of Edwin Lewis Snyder. But the real treat comes as Tamalpais swings to the left, beneath heavy shade, and reveals the storybook cottage on the right at 149. This enchanted cottage, called "one of the most romantic and rustic homes in Berkeley" by the Berkeley Architectural Heritage Association, dates from 1906 and includes later additions from designer John Hudson Thomas.

Just past this wooden delight, you will find the top of Tamalpais Path. Turn right and descend, using the handrails, this most magnificent of staircases. Drop down a steep 183 steps, over many landings, through a shady dell, admiring the fine woods to your right and the graffiti to your left. You may also note a path and a gate on your right. These lead to one of the area's most charming spots—a small waterfall section of Codornices Creek. It is privately owned, but I am assured the owner does not mind the occasional visitor taking a respectful look. Walk lightly and, as they say, take nothing but photographs and leave nothing but footprints.

Continuing down, the stairs end in an elegant half-spiral twist and deposit you on the back side of Codornices Park.

Bear right, and cross the little wooden bridge over Codornices Creek. Rise up the pathway, with the park on your left and Euclid dead ahead. There you will find your starting point.

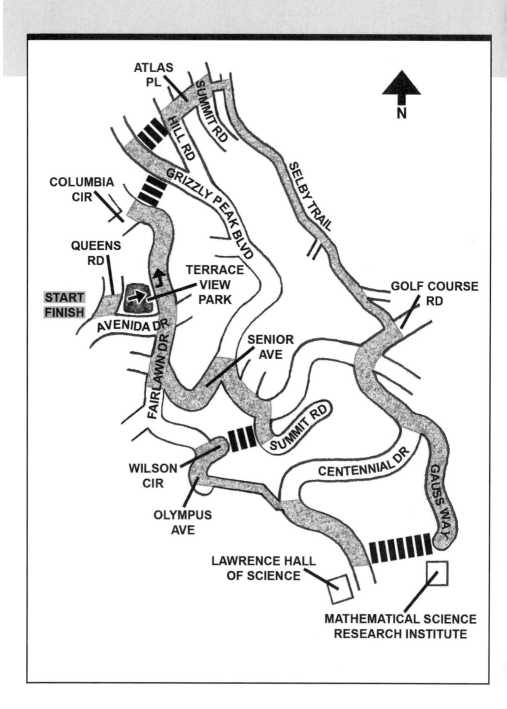

WALK #11

TERRACE VIEW PARK
DURATION: **1 hour, 15 minutes**
DISTANCE: **2.3 miles**
STEPS: **544**
DIFFICULTY: **3.5–4**
BUS: **65, 67**

This is a strenuous walk, part stairs, part hiking trail, that offers the biggest views in the Berkeley hills. While not recommended in wet or muddy weather, it is a stunner at sunset— particularly if you start the walk 45 minutes before the sun goes down. For an even more massive workout, do this walk backwards, from finish to start.

Begin your walk at Terrace View Park, high above Berkeley, off Queens Road, near the intersection of Queens and Avenida Drive. Walk up the sloping driveway into the park. Bear right, and take nine steps and a walkway up to a flat area, then pass a swing set and cross a grassy lawn. Take 35 more stairs up, and land on Fairlawn Drive. Take a left and walk along a short stretch. It doesn't last long. Soon, on your right, you will find the next set of steps.

These stairs might be mistaken for private steps, if not for the "Columbia Walk" signpost. Turn in, and up. This walkway begins as seven steps up onto a resident's side yard, where it crosses a brick patio, rises six more wooden steps, and becomes a path into the trees. Stay on the right, close to the fence, until the path becomes a set of 30 railroad tie steps rising out of the trees and up onto Grizzly Peak Boulevard.

This is a busy piece of roadway, and the cars move fast. Cross very carefully, then turn left, and downhill. Then, in front of the house at 1311, turn up and into the driveway. It doesn't look like a public pathway, I know, but it is. (There's a public marker before the driveway, but it's hardly visible, and usually overlooked.) Climb the driveway. At the top, find the staircase rising to your left.

This is a steep, steep collection of railroad tie risers, climbing 40 steps to a very welcome bench. Stop, sit, and observe the splendors below—Berkeley, the Berkeley Marina, Cesar Chavez Park, Alcatraz, Angel Island, the Golden Gate Bridge.... Then get up and climb on, another 47 railroad tie steps to the top of the hill.

But don't stop there! You arrive at Hill Road and Atlas Place. Walk straight ahead onto Atlas. Where it meets Summit Road, continue straight ahead. You'll see a "Not A Through Street" sign on the left. Just beside that, find the pathway that goes up and over a little hummock. Walk down and right onto Selby Trail.

Hike along this charming woodland walkway, enjoying views to your left of a golf course and the parts of Tilden Park that surround it. The path will continue for quite a while—a half a mile, just about—as it rises to a bench dedicated to one Dorothy Mozen. Don't turn right and uphill here. Continue straight ahead as the trail winds down and to the left, then rises again.

In time you will see a roadway below, and the path will fork. Aim ahead and right, following the contour of the hill as the trail drops down toward the road. When you reach it, cross it—for the record, it's Golf Course Road—and turn right. Walk uphill to the intersection with Grizzly Peak Boulevard, and cross carefully. Continue on the other side, as Golf Course Road becomes Centennial Drive.

Centennial bends and descends to the right. Follow it a short distance, to the first turning, and take the left onto Gauss Way. Follow this past the parking lots on the left and the stand of massive eucalyptus on the right, climbing a short hill and

Shaded steps of stone in the Berkeley hills.

walking between the buildings of the Space Science Laboratory. Walk straight on, until the road "T"s. Turn right, and walk along the front of the Mathematical Sciences Research Institute and Shiing-Shin Chern Hall. Veer slightly to the right as you pass this building, and aim for a wooden handrail visible off to the right. Then take 15 steps down and stop. Be amazed. Go faint with delight. Then take 16 more steps down, find a redwood bench, and try to recover.

This may not be Berkeley's *best* view, but it's certainly its *biggest*. From here the entire East Bay lies stretched out like Eliot's etherized patient. The views extend from Oakland International Airport to the south, to Point Richmond and the San Rafael Bridge to the north, with the city of San Francisco, the Sutro tower, and the Golden Gate Bridge dead ahead. (I'm told you can even see the Farallon Islands on a clear day, past the Golden Gate, but they're 27 miles off shore, so it would have to be a *very* clear day.) Directly below, much closer in, is the Lawrence Hall of Science. That's the sand-colored, space-age adobe structure in the foreground, and that's where you're headed next.

When you've had enough of the view—is there *ever* enough, really?—collect yourself and begin the long descent to the Lawrence Hall of Science parking lots. (They also serve as overflow parking lots on Cal game days. Maybe that's why they're so huge.) It's a long way down. You fall a total of 199 steps, plus the 31 you already walked down, across many levels of parking lot, to land ultimately on Centennial once again. Cross the street with the light at the crosswalk. If you have time, and interest, turn left and check out the Hall of Science. If not, turn right, walk until you can turn left into a parking lot, and stay to the right as the parking lot hugs the cliffs and gives off more great views of Berkeley and the bay.

At the end of the parking lot, a narrow trail peels off to the left. Follow this until you see a metal gate on the right and, beyond it, a roadway. Turn in there. Walk a half block of Olympus Avenue, then turn right almost at once onto Wilson Circle.

Climb up to the end of this cul-de-sac street. Dead ahead, find Wilson Path.

It's the last climb, and it's serious: 105 redwood railroad ties, straight up the side of the hill, to deposit you panting on Summit Road—the same Summit Road you crossed near the middle of this walk. Take a left onto Summit. Walk a short block. Take a left onto Grizzly Peak. Then take another left, quite soon, onto Senior Avenue.

This will descend rapidly and hit Fairlawn. Turn right, and walk along Fairlawn as it descends even more. Cross Avenida carefully at the stop sign. Just ahead, on your left, you'll find the top side of Terrace View Park. Take the 26 steps down into the park. Turn toward the swing set. Grab the walkway with nine steps down to the driveway. Take the driveway back to Queens Road, and your starting point.

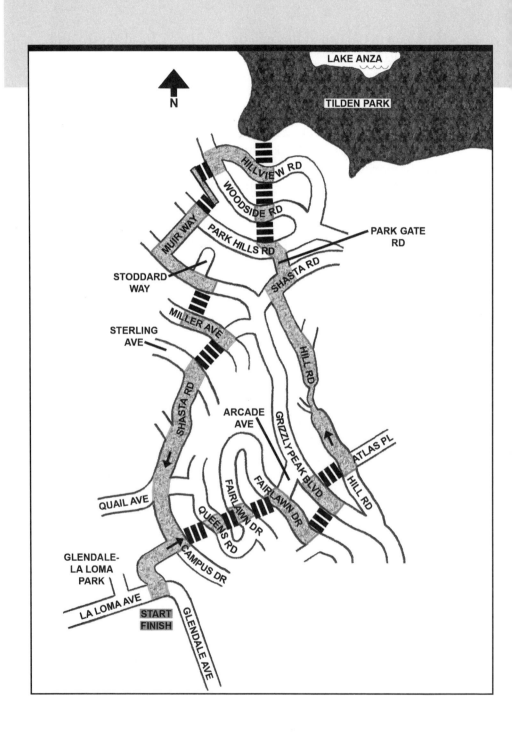

WALK #12

GRIZZLY PEAKS
DURATION: **1 hour, 30 minutes**
DISTANCE: **2.5 miles**
STEPS: **941**
DIFFICULTY: **5**
BUS: **65, 67**

This is a giant walk, or hike, and is one of the most vigorous in this collection. But what a climb! It offers deeply shaded canyon staircases, towering views, and almost total solitude.

Begin your walk from the stunning Glendale-La Loma Park, high above East Berkeley, near where the streets of those two names meet. There is ample parking, a fine grassy ball field, and restrooms at the field level. When you're ready, leave the park and walk uphill on Glendale to the "T" intersection with Campus Drive. Directly ahead is your first set of stairs.

This is the Glendale Path. It starts with a steep set of 33 concrete steps, with handrails, rising under a canopy of redwoods, and then becomes a dirt path interrupted by railroad ties—38 of them as you climb. A plaque along the way explains that you are near the source of Codornices Creek, should that interest you. (It does not explain that "codornices," in Spanish, means "quails." Apparently the birds were quite abundant when Spanish-speaking settlers first arrived.) Beyond the plaque, the railroad tie steps resume, and lift you another 62 steps up the narrow canyon.

At the top, you land on Queens Road. Cross this and find the steps that resume on the other side. Climb up 19 railroad tie steps to a dirt path that rises through a very low ceiling of trees and vines. Beyond that, the railroad ties continue for another 21 steps—some of them a little unsteady—to deposit you on Fairlawn Drive.

Cross Fairlawn and continue up Glendale Path. This is the last third of the pathway. It begins with a sharp 53 concrete steps up, where you may pause at another informational plaque. This one discusses the 100-million-year-old rock you're hiking on. Then the railroad tie steps resume, up five steps to a dirt path that culminates in a fine wide stone staircase of 13 steps. You arrive at last at the intersection of Fairlawn and Arcade Avenue.

Turn right, following Fairlawn, along a nice woody block. Shortly on your left, just after the house at 151, you will find the next set of steps. (These might be mistaken for private steps, if not for the "Columbia Walk" signpost, and a small plaque acknowledging a local Eagle Scout for the hard work he did building the staircase in 2005.) They begin as seven steps up into the residence's side yard, where they cross a brick patio, climb six wood steps, and continue. Stay well to the right, hugging the fence, as the path rises under redwood overhang to a set of 30 railroad tie steps. These deposit you on Grizzly Peak Boulevard.

But you're not finished climbing—not hardly. Watch out for the traffic on this fast-moving boulevard. Then turn left and walk slightly downhill. Just after the house at 1321, you'll catch sight of the "Atlas Path" sign on the right side of the road. Paying close attention here, walk to the next driveway, for 1311 Grizzly Peak, and turn in. Walk up the driveway—trust me, this *is* the path—and at the top find the stairway going up beside the house. You'll climb 40 steps, going up a steep hillside, before you arrive at a strategically placed bench. Sit and be amazed: Below you are the city, the bay, the Golden Gate Bridge, Mount Tamalpais, and more.

When you've caught your breath, resume hiking. Climb a total of 47 more steps to land at the corner of Hill Road and Atlas Place. Turn left, heading downhill on Hill, admiring the topiary bushes on your right, and continue until the pavement ends. Do not fail, in your exhaustion, to appreciate the huge views here, but proceed carefully. Enter the driveway straight ahead, between the houses at 80 and 90, veer slightly to the left and head down, approximately 30 paces. Then, on the right, find the tiny dirt track half-hidden in the bushes.

This is Scott Newhall Path, named after the longtime Berkeley resident and Cal grad who went on to edit the *San Francisco Chronicle*. He later retired in Newhall, the Los Angeles suburb founded by his grandfather that bears the family name. Follow this along as it hugs the hillside and passes through a chain link gate, passing under low-hanging oaks, until the pavement resumes. You are on the other side of Hill Road now. Head left down the road and down the hill, and stay on the left where the road forms a "Y."

At the bottom, Hill flattens and runs into Shasta Road. Turn right onto Shasta, then turn left at once onto Park Gate Road and walk straight ahead toward the fountain and the gates that read "Park Hills." This looks like a private housing development—it was developed in the 1940s as part of Contra Costa County, but was later transferred to Berkeley and annexed to Alameda County, and is overseen by the Park Hills Neighborhood Association—but the streets and pathways are open to the public. Stay on the left side, go through the gates, and stop where Shasta meets Park Hills Road. Right in front of you should be a sign for Fred Herbert Path.

Enter the pathway—named after a former Park Hills resident of that name, who was a president of the homeowners' association and known as Mr. Park Hills—descend 42 railroad tie steps to a shady, curving pathway, then drop 40 more stairs. Cross a flat patch of yard, go through a chain link gate, and drop down 24 steps more. Land on Woodside Drive, cross the road, and resume the Fred Herbert Path. Descend 24 railroad tie steps down a wide, shady walk, and then descend 70 steps more. This will deposit you on Hillview Road. Cross the street, and continue on down a final 64 railroad tie steps.

You're now at the edge of marvelous Tilden Park. If you walk a few feet to your left and stare out through the redwoods, you can see the shining green surface of Lake Anza. If it's hot, and you're bold, you can bushwhack straight ahead down the hill and land more or less in the water, where swimming from a public beach is allowed. If it's not hot, or *you're* not, turn around and walk back up the 64 steps to Hillview Road. Turn right, walk a block, and bear slightly left onto Woodside Road. Look at once for the pathway on the right, between the houses at 1088 and 1100 Woodside. This is Muir Path.

Start up through a shady glen, up seven steps and onto a paved sloping path. And beware: The first time I walked here I surprised a deer dining in the underbrush. He leapt over a fence, into a yard, and disappeared. Where the path meets a grassy stretch of parkland, bear left and uphill. Near the top of the grass, you will see gas and water pipes up and to the right. Aim for that, and find the other end of Muir Path extending up between two houses. Take 24 steps up, with a steep finish, and land on Muir Way.

Walk straight ahead for one block, then turn left onto Grizzly Peak again. Now, I am happy to say, you have no more climbing ahead of you. Being mindful of the traffic, and using the crosswalk to get to the other side, cross Grizzly Peak. Walk past the left-hand turning for Stoddard Way. Then, on the right, just after the house at 1160, find Stoddard Path. Turn in and begin your first big descent down a path that cuts between two houses, gets steeper, and ends in 71 stairs that drop you at 1165 Miller Avenue. Turn left and walk along a stretch of refreshingly flat road.

At the stop sign, where Miller meets Shasta, find your final staircase—on the right, coming in just past the stop sign. This is Shasta Path. It drops a very steep 137 railroad tie steps, beneath a shady overhang, and concludes on another curve of

Shasta Avenue. To the right is Sterling Avenue. Ignore this, but walk instead straight ahead, downhill on Shasta. At the first corner, Shasta will peel off to the right, and the road ahead will become Campus Drive. Go straight. At the second corner, you'll cross Quail Avenue. Continue straight. Soon you will come to the intersection of Campus and Glendale. The first staircase you climbed will be on your left. Turn right, and head downhill. Enter the driveway for Glendale-La Loma Park to return to your starting point.

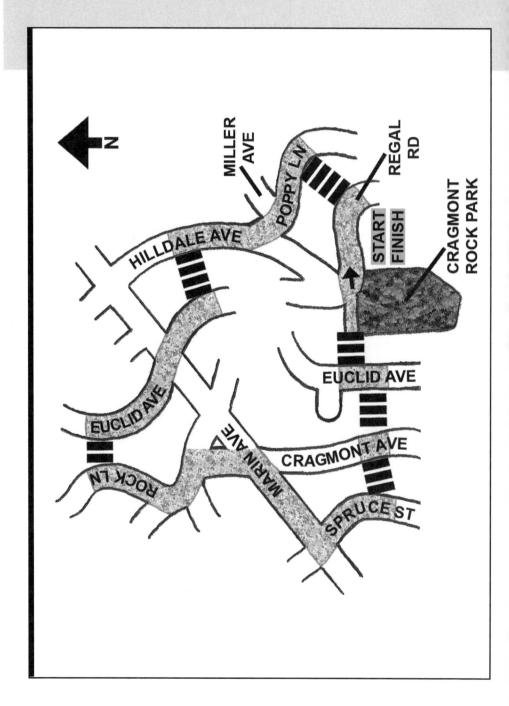

WALK #13

CRAGMONT ROCK PARK
DURATION: **45 minutes**
DISTANCE: **1.5 miles**
STEPS: **301**
DIFFICULTY: **2.5–3**
BUS: **65, 67**

This is a relatively short walk through a charming hillside neighborhood, beginning and ending in a small park that is ideal for a lunchtime or sunset picnic.

Start your walk in the upper Northbrae area, off Marin Avenue, near Cragmont Rock Park. Take a minute to admire its fine bay views, grassy lawns, and shaded picnic table. Then return to the front of the park, near the corner of Regal Road and Hilldale Avenue. Start walking east on Regal, away from Hilldale, with the park on your right. Half a block down the hill, just after the house at 979, find the unmarked Pinnacle Path on your left.

This is a charming staircase that rises eight steps past a mosaic tile tribute to a local woman named Irene Juniper. A walkway slopes up past the tile and climbs through a leafy overhang to another 14 steps, then delivers you to 58 Poppy Lane. Take a left and walk uphill slightly, past an imposing concrete home at 37, and past the turning for Miller Avenue. As the road descends, meet Hilldale again and bear right onto it. Just after the house at 920, beside a small mound of flowering lavender, find the next staircase on your left.

This is a fine newer structure, locally known as Billie Jean Walk, with sturdy handrails on both sides and a low overhang of power lines. Descend 66 steps, over several landings, past a good-looking flower and vegetable garden on the left, and a bamboo forest on the right. Finish with a final series of 77 steeper steps to land next to 917 Euclid Avenue.

Turn right and walk to the corner, taking advantage of the tiny three-step staircase that serves the bus stop. Cross busy Marin Avenue, continuing on Euclid, and cross to the western side of the street. Here you'll find a sidewalk running just below street level, and a strange Stonehenge-like *menhir* or *dolmen* in front of the house at 834. A short bit later, after the house at 810, find marked Rock Walk on your left.

Descend again, down a group of 27 steps separated by lengths of sloping sidewalk, to land at 46 Rock Lane. Turn left. Enjoy the spreading bay views, with the Port of Oakland directly ahead, and admire the inset glass design on the garage at 14, as you drop down Rock. At the corner, where you meet Cragmont Avenue, turn left.

Follow Cragmont across Regal Road and, at the next corner, cross the street and turn right down Marin. Let your quads do some work as you descend past the striking Cragmont Elementary on your right. At the first corner, turn left onto Spruce Street. Walk down a block's length and then, after the house at 933, find the delightful Easter Way.

This is a wide, elegant set of stairs, said to have been the pathway used by pilgrims who, in the thousands, climbed this hill at sunrise to participate in Easter morning religious services at Cragmont Rock Park. It begins with four double-wide risers, under deep oaky shade, that give onto a wide rising slope interrupted at intervals by sets of stairs—25 in total. Soon the stairs are outfitted with a center handrail, and rise another set of 34 steps to the sidewalk, and an additional three to the street, to drop you back onto Cragmont.

Cross the street, taking note of the funicular trashcan

railway just to your left, then find the next stretch of Easter Way dead ahead. This is another fine mix of stairs and sloping side-walk, a climb of 40 steps in all, under the shade of redwoods and a loquat tree, that delivers you once again to Euclid.

Cross the street here, too, and turn left. Just past the bus stop, and just before the driveway for 971, find the last stretch of Easter Way on the right. Take three steps up, and then a long sloping sidewalk, past the beautiful old shingled-style home at 975 Euclid on the right. This passes the falling lawns of Crag-mont Rock Park before arriving shortly at Regal Road again. You are now back at the park and your starting point.

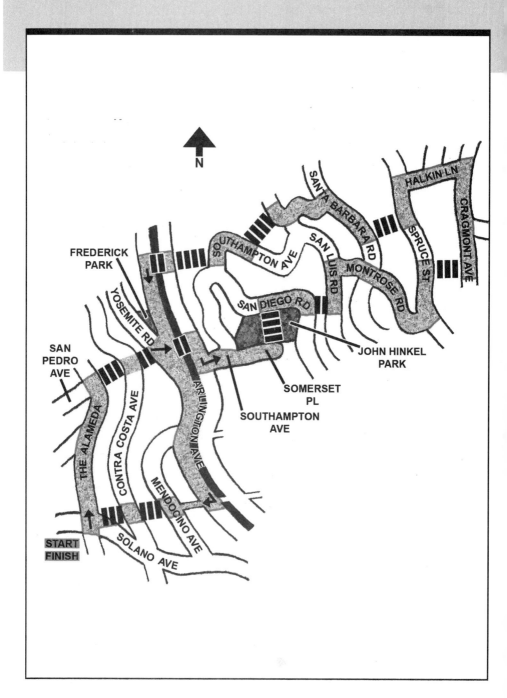

WALK #14

NORTHBRAE HEIGHTS
DURATION: **1 hour, 30 minutes**
DISTANCE: **2.8 miles**
STEPS: **446**
DIFFICULTY: **4**
BUS: **18, 25**

This is a fine hillside climb, over many staircases, rising high into the hills of Northbrae. It delivers fine bay views and a tour of some even finer local architecture.

Begin your walk in the Northeast Berkeley section known as Thousand Oaks, near the intersection of Solano Avenue and The Alameda, perhaps with a cup of mud at either Starbucks or Peet's. If you're hungry, grab a bit of bakery at La Farine or a slice at Zachary's, an employee-owned pizzeria popular with locals. Admire the historic Oaks Theater as you pass. Then start walking north along The Alameda. After two blocks, where San Pedro Avenue comes in on the left, find your first staircase on the right.

This is the Yosemite Steps, which begins as a sloping sidewalk and three short steps, running narrowly between houses, passing a delightful backyard garden and "stream" on the left, before taking 19 steps up and depositing you at 800 Contra Costa Avenue. Jog a few paces to the right, cross the street, and continue up the next section of Yosemite. You'll climb 15 steps, helped by a heavy steel handrail, then hit a slope that will culminate in 28 steps up to the corner of Yosemite Road and Arlington Avenue.

In front of you is tiny Frederick Park, a quaint bit of land given to the city in 1921 by J. F. Hink, a department store owner whose dry goods business once occupied the ground floor of the historic Shattuck Hotel. Ahead to the right is a crosswalk. Take that, and the 21 stairs involved, to carefully cross the divided Arlington and obtain the elevated sidewalk on the other side. Turn right and head downhill, and then turn left again almost at once into Southampton Avenue. Half a block up, at

A FOGGY VIEW OF THE BAY FROM HIGH IN THE BERKELEY HILLS.

the "Y" intersection of Southampton and Somerset Place, bear right onto Somerset. Follow the line of the park to the cul-de-sac with the huge oak in the middle—taking note of the fine old Spanish house at 38 Somerset, a walled 1925 compound from local designer Noble Newsom—and continue around the park to a small stone amphitheater.

This was once the heart of John Hinkel Park, the seven-acre recreation area named after the Berkeley philanthropist who lived on nearby Channing Way, and who donated the park land to the city in 1919. The amphitheater, built in 1934 as a WPA project from plans drawn by the same Vernon Dean who designed the Berkeley Rose Garden, once hosted community theater, barbershop quartets, folk music festivals, and until the early 1990s, the Berkeley Shakespeare Festival. (The organization behind it, Cal Shakes, is still going strong, but is based in Orinda. The theater is used for various activities during the summer.) Next to this you will find a series of stone steps climbing up the hill into the spreading shade.

Climb 64 steps up to a flat platform where several paths meet—you will see many paths, winding through the park—just below a derelict wooden structure that was once the John Hinkel Park clubhouse. Enjoy the oaky, redwoody shade and the squirrels playing overhead, then take the path straight ahead and up, over 15 railroad tie steps. Then turn right onto the asphalt path. Walk up and over, past the little waterfall, being mindful of your footing if it's wet. Turn left and take 23 stone steps, then turn left again and take 21 more. You land across the street from 767 San Diego Road.

Turn right. To your left are two mid-century modernist houses at 771 and 775—both designs from former Cal architecture professor Donald Olsen. Past these and up the hill, find narrow Upton Lane across the street on your left. Take seven stone steps, with rails, to a narrow sloping path, through a canopy of bamboo, and finish with a group of 42 more to land at 768 San Luis Road.

Turn left, walk a short block to Montrose Road, and then

turn right. Climb up, admiring the increasingly larger homes and gardens, across Santa Barbara Road. As the road crests and flattens, you will meet busy Spruce Street. Turn left and cross the street, and on the right find the next set of stairs between the houses at 747 and 743 Spruce.

This is Poplar Path. Climb 25 risers, with a welcome handrail, to a sloping sidewalk ending with 14 more steps and landing at 757 Cragmont Avenue. Turn left onto Cragmont, walk past the right turn for Poplar Street, and be happy that you have no more climbing to do. Instead, walk to the corner and turn left and downhill onto Halkin Lane.

Some maps show a planned or abandoned pathway running from Halkin Lane *uphill* to the right, connecting it to Euclid. I wasn't able to find this, and a local woman tending her garden told me the pathway had never been built—though the Berkeley Path Wanderers Association has plans to create one.

So head downhill on Halkin instead, enjoying grand views west across the bay. You shortly meet Spruce again. Cross the street and turn left, and admire the startling statuary in front of the house at 707—home to the ceramist whose work you see. Then look to the right to find Alta Vista Path, just after the large red-tiled Spanish home at 710. This staircase drops two steps down from the street, then another 11, and slopes down gently until dropping a final 86 steep stairs—and giving you big western views as you go.

You land across from 728 Santa Barbara. (This was once the home of Navy Admiral Chester Nimitz, who after World War II moved to Berkeley and became a UC Regent.) Cross the street and turn right, heading downhill. Turn left on Southampton, just past the huge copper-colored mansion at 260 Southampton. Go one block, and turn right onto San Luis Road. Then, just ahead on your left, find Chester Lane (named after the Admiral, perhaps) right after the house at 690.

Chester drops nine little steps onto a narrow shady path, bordered by lush gardens and a row of olive trees. It's an oasis of cool and quiet, and deposits you on Southampton Avenue once more. Turn right, and admire the hens and roosters in the yard at 116—where you'll also see a sculpture of a mother bear and her cubs, a W. W. Dixon building from 1927. Note also the Spanish masterpiece across the street at 117, a Williams & Wastell design from the same year. Then begin to look on your right for the next staircase, known as Tunbridge Lane, just after the house at 101. This falls 25 steep steps and leads you down another lovely shaded corridor overhung heavily with shrubs and vines.

You land on Arlington again. Take 13 steps down to the sidewalk, five more to the crosswalk, 11 more as you split the middle of the busy, divided road, and then turn left on the opposite sidewalk, heading downhill. There are more fine views here, between the houses, of the bay and the Golden Gate Bridge.

Walk past Frederick Park and Yosemite Road. Walk past the rock bridge that runs over Blackberry Creek, and past the turning for Mendocino Avenue—pausing perhaps to appreciate the enormous estate with the ornate gate on the corner, a William Milwain home, set on several lots, built in 1923. Then note the Julia Morgan home at 872 with its stucco-and-shingle combination and leaded-glass windows, and another at 883, with its three-gabled roof.

Just before the house at 900 Arlington, by a grove of fine redwoods, turn right into the hidden Indian Rock Path. (Behind that grove, at 892, is the Kay House, another example of John Hudson Thomas' work.) This narrow passage will lead you between two charming houses and carry you downhill to Mendocino. Cross the street and continue for another length of the pathway, and land, after six little steps, on Contra Costa Avenue. For a diversion, turn right and walk half a block to Contra Costa Rock, and the "park" that surrounds it. Like Indian Rock, it's a huge lump of half-buried stone, into which steps have been carved. You can climb the rock and get some fine views of the bay.

Return to Indian Rock Path and continue downhill. The path will slope down to a final four steps, and drop you at the corner of The Alameda and Solano—back at your starting point.

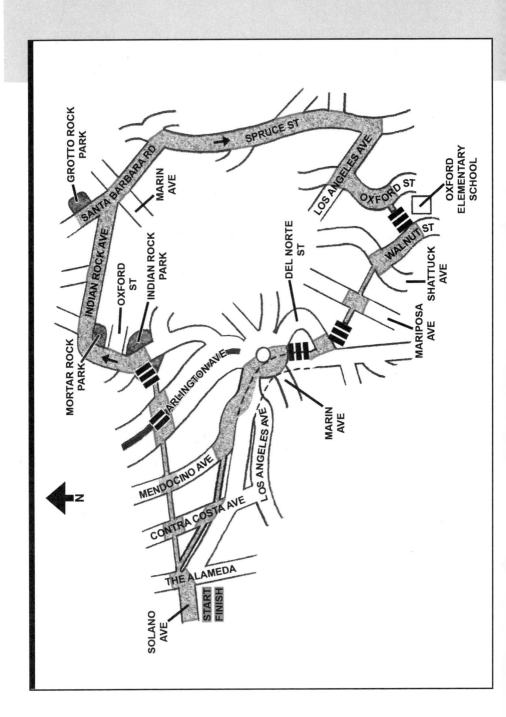

WALK #15

NORTHBRAE ROCK PATHS
DURATION: **1 hour, 15 minutes**
DISTANCE: **2.3 miles**
STEPS: **87**
DIFFICULTY: **2.5**
BUS: **18, 25**

This is a gentle walk involving relatively few stairs but many walkways, and a huge serving of fine architecture. Most of the streets and lots you'll pass were laid out by the Mason-McDuffie Co. after the 1906 earthquake, to take advantage of the flight of San Francisco families moving to the East Bay. The neighborhoods are still lovely, 100 years later.

Begin your walk in the Thousand Oaks commercial district near The Alameda and Solano Avenue, perhaps with a snack from one of the many ethnic eateries nearby or a screening at the historic Oaks Theater. Then walk up Solano, cross The Alameda, and on the northeast corner climb four steps onto Indian Rock Path, heading uphill right out of the intersection.

This is the first leg of a long walkway that was designed to give the hillside residents a shortcut down to the electric street car that ran from Shattuck Avenue in Berkeley onto Solano Avenue in Northbrae. Walk closely between the houses as the walkway arrives at Contra Costa Avenue, crosses the street, rises six steps, and continues up the slope. Here is the first of many fine Japanese maples that turn gold in autumn, as well as ginger flowers and a profusion of morning glory.

Cross Mendocino Avenue, and continue up the next leg

to Arlington Avenue. Use 11 steps to cross to the uphill side of this very busy divided road, then nine more to continue up the path. Shortly ahead, the path runs smack into Indian Rock.

A nearby plaque informs you that the original developers of the area "donated" parcels of land to be turned into community park space, perhaps making a virtue of necessity—the donated parcels all are occupied by enormous rocks. Ahead you will find many such park spaces. Each of them is, basically, a single, giant rock.

For now, head left past Indian Rock and use the 23 stone steps to climb up and around. Amuse yourself if you like by climbing the rock, on which Depression-era mountaineers are said to have trained for bigger ascents. It's a popular park for amateur climbers, with their pitons and carabiners, and for local folks who arrive at sunset with picnic baskets, bottles of wine, and acoustic guitars. Or cross the street into the grassy area of Indian Rock Park, where there are welcome benches. (Overhead, you'll note an old air raid siren.) If you're an architecture buff, walk downhill a bit. The big house on your left at the corner of Indian Rock and Shattuck is a good example of the work of John Hudson Thomas, a 1911 design known as the Pratt-Thomas House. The two houses to its right are also Thomas homes. Together, the collection is sometimes referred to as "The Three Sisters."

When you're done, turn around and walk back uphill on Indian Rock Avenue. Enjoy another Thomas house, the big green Fleager House on your right, at 927. Pass Oxford Street, admiring the huge stone pillar that used to serve as the area's street sign—all of Northbrae's main street corners used to feature these attractive markers—and follow Indian Rock to the right, around the corner, as it brushes up against another rock park. (This one is Mortar Rock Park. Study the rocks closely and you can find the carved bowls where the first residents, the local Ohlone Indians, ground acorns into meal.) The collection of native plants is the work of Friends of Five Creeks, a local volunteer group dedicated to preserving natural habitats by removing invasive plant species and replacing them with hardy home-grown varieties.

Continue east on Indian Rock, gaining altitude and increasingly pleasant views as you go. Note the fine Craftsman homes, some with redwood shingle siding, and pause to appreciate the goat that can sometimes be seen trimming the hillside. Note the nice iron fencing at 805, too.

Up to your left there is yet another rock park, this one called Grotto Rock Park. It also offers stairs that rise to a good view. Check that out, then turn right onto Santa Barbara Road, and then cross busy Marin Avenue with the crosswalk. Continue along Santa Barbara, passing an impressive collection of redwood trees on your left just before you meet Spruce Street. Turn right onto Spruce, and head downhill.

There is a lot to see here—big fine houses, an architectural mixed bag of styles, from hexagonal modernist to historic Craftsman and, after San Benito, some nice views of the bay between the houses. Note the big carved bear with two bear cubs in the yard at 1086, and the huge chalet-style house on the corner of Spruce and Los Angeles, which has recently undergone a massive restoration.

Turn right, just after that house, onto Los Angeles, and then take the first left onto Oxford. This quiet street will descend and flatten. After a few hundred feet, and the house at 1128, look for the short cut known as "The Short Cut." Turn right just before you hit the Oxford Elementary School, which has operated on this site since 1910.

The Short Cut is a narrow corridor passing between some houses and the school yard. It drops down nine steps, eventually, and deposits you onto Walnut Street. Turn right, and at the "T" intersection with Shattuck Avenue, cross the street and go straight ahead—straight into the delightful Terrace Walk.

This is a charming lane, lined with houses whose front doors and windows face the walkway, and through whose front yards you are now walking. (The "Wright House," at 21 Terrace Walk, is said to be another John Hudson Thomas design, from

1912. The lovely wooden barn at 81, too, is worth a look.) Cross Mariposa Avenue, a favorite avenue among local walkers, who report that it is often used for movie shoots, and is always closed and decorated extensively for Halloween. Then continue on to the second length of Terrace Walk. Here you may pause to admire the fine rose garden at number 30. The very friendly occupant here planted all 120 rose bushes, she told me, over her 40 years in the house. Many of them are individually named ("Big Ben," "Billie Jean," etc.) and all are lovely.

Terrace Walk concludes with six steps down onto a complicated intersection where, in the old days, street car passengers could transfer from the line running into Northbrae and another heading down Hopkins. The old storefronts across the street once were home to a bakery and a corner grocery. To navigate the intersection, walk directly ahead, using the crosswalk to cross Del Norte Street, and aim for the broad stone staircase in front of you.

This is the beginning of Fountain Walk, which is the pedestrian alternative to the section of Solano Avenue that runs through the tunnel ahead and out into the Thousand Oaks neighborhood. The tunnel was built in 1910, and was big enough for an electric street car that ran until at least the 1940s, when it was converted for use by automobiles. It also includes a sidewalk, but...why go there? Instead, climb the 19 steep steps up to a sloping walkway, lined with an ornate Italianate balustrade, which carries you up and over the hill.

At the top, you will find an even more complicated intersection. This is "The Circle," where seven boulevards meet. Each of them is named after a large California county—San Diego, San Mateo, Yolo, etc. The design and choice of names were the result of a campaign by the Northbrae developers in 1908 to move the California state capitol from Sacramento to North Berkeley. The campaign failed, obviously, but the street names remain. The fountain, which features a group of grizzly bear cubs playing in the water, was designed by John Galen Howard, founder of UC Berkeley's school of architecture and the designer of iconic Cal structures like the Campanile, Sather Gate, and the Greek Theater.

To navigate this complex roundabout, go clockwise to your left. Use the crosswalk to pass Marin, then Los Angeles, and then immediately turn left down Mendocino. (It looks like the other half of Los Angeles, but is its own street.) Follow this downhill, past some fine old homes on the right, noting the other side of the tunnel below you on the left. Just before the house at 928, find the top of Black Path.

This asphalt walkway drops down and parallels Solano, past one more huge outcropping of raw stone. It will pass Contra Costa Avenue, and land you at the intersection of Solano and The Alameda, at the bottom of Indian Rock Path, and back at your starting point.

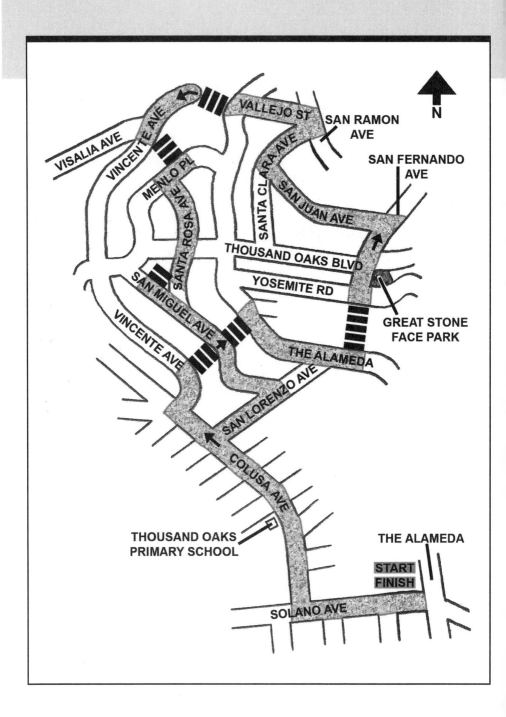

WALK #16

GREAT STONE FACE PARK
DURATION: **1 hour, 15 minutes**
DISTANCE: **2.3 miles**
STEPS: **336**
DIFFICULTY: **2.5–3**
BUS: **18, 25**

This is another shorter walk, and an architectural smorgasbord of classic Berkeley builders, which rises from the flats of Solano Avenue into some of the most picturesque staircases the East Bay has to offer.

Begin your journey in North Berkeley, near the Thousand Oaks area and the intersection of Solano Avenue and The Alameda. After a caffeine injection or a snack from La Farine, Noah's Bagels, or one of the area's other eateries, leave the busy Solano commercial block and head north on Colusa Avenue.

Walk past the sprawling Thousand Oaks Elementary School, and cross the turnings for Tacoma, Capistrano, and San Lorenzo, pausing just a bit perhaps to admire the gently flowing Capistrano Creek and the pleasant oak trees shading it. A little further on, turn right onto Vincente Avenue. Check out the massive stone outcropping at 683, where builders made the best of the boulders and carved a charming walkway into the stone. Then, one house further on, find your first staircase on the right.

This is El Paseo Path. It starts with four big heavy stone

steps up, onto a sloping walkway interrupted by a series of 33 more stone steps. Note the stone as you go. The steps are chunks of the rock removed to make way for the houses, and this area is teeming with staircases, retaining walls and garden ornamentation built from the same stone. Note too the profusion of back yard incinerators on this stretch of walkway. You can almost smell the burning leaves.

You land on San Miguel Avenue. Directly across the street is the continuation of El Paseo Path. Enter here, up more of the same heavy stone risers, and climb another 16 steps that rise past one huge chunk of stone that the builders left behind. (You can see some marks where pieces of it were removed, perhaps to cut the stones you've been stepping up.) At the top of the walk you land at 646 The Alameda. For a treat, walk up to the left slightly and admire the remarkable use of stone at 641. The front yard is one massive boulder, with the house and garage set back behind it. That done, turn the other way, and walk downhill on The Alameda.

As the street bottoms out, and San Lorenzo Avenue comes in on the right, pay close attention. Under a profusion of low-hanging oak, you'll find the entrance to Indian Trail on your left, just past an oversized stone urn.

Ornamental urns of this kind were once the symbolic mascot of the Thousand Oaks neighborhood, and the important intersections were marked with them when the subdivision was laid out in 1909. For the last couple of years, the Thousand Oaks Neighborhood Association has been raising funds to build new urns and install them in their original locations.

Indian Trail is a rustic climb, a winding trail that rises on heavy stone steps set in the oaky hillside. A haven for squirrels and blue jays, the path climbs 90 steps, separated by pathway, past the remarkable brick-and-shingle structure on the left—a Henry Higby Gutterson house dating from 1915.

At the top you arrive at last on Yosemite Road, at the intersection with San Fernando Avenue. To your immediate left is the Robert C. Newell House, said to be the first residence ever

Stairs cut in ancient stone at Indian Rock Park.

built in Thousand Oaks. To your immediate right is the Robert Leavens House, a Walter Steilberg home featuring that architect's signature green Chinese tiles. And just across the street is Great Stone Face Park, another of this area's marvelously stoney public areas. This one offers a fine shady picnic table, a welcome water fountain, paths that wander through the rocks, and no indication whatsoever why it is called Great Stone Face Park. If you find the correct angle, I am told, you can see the great stone face itself—no, not Buster Keaton, though he had that nickname in his lifetime—looking skyward, its chin down and to the left, its nose and forehead up and to the right.

When you've enjoyed yourself sufficiently, leave the park and walk uphill onto San Fernando. Directly across the street, take note of the house at 686 San Fernando, which is a 1930 Tudor Revival design from local architects Sidney and Noble Newsom. Kitty corner from there, across Thousand Oaks Boulevard, you may admire the leaded glass windows on another Newsom house at 1923 Thousand Oaks.

Walk a block north on San Fernando, then turn left onto San Juan Avenue. Here the oak trees thicken, and the profusion of fine old homes continues. As you walk on, pay particular attention to the homes at 1831 and 1827—the first, a William Hays Shingle-style from 1914 that has undergone some modern adjustments, and the second, a Bernard Maybeck from the year after.

Where San Juan slopes down and meets Santa Clara Avenue, turn right and head uphill a very short block. Then turn left onto San Ramon Avenue, and left again immediately onto Vallejo Street. Drop down a block, noting the fine fern garden on the left, and the fine big shingle-sided home on the right. Then, directly ahead, where Vallejo meets The Alameda, find your next staircase.

This is Vincente Walk, an extremely picturesque descent of 88 steps, over multiple landings, under oaky overhang, that drops to the cul-de-sac end of Vincente Avenue. Turn left, and head downhill on the elevated sidewalk on the left-hand side, enjoying this quiet, leafy canyon. As the sidewalk ends, drop down eight more steps to street level, and continue downhill.

Where Vincente meets Visalia on the right, just past another example of builders using boulders at 495, find Visalia Steps rising on the left. This offers a fine view of the bay and the mountains of Marin County. Like its cousin Vincente, this is a delightful, stony stretch of steps, rising a total of 87 rock risers through a heavy oak overhang, to land on Menlo Place.

Turn right. Walk past the charming oak tree, standing in solitary duty in the very middle of the street, and turn left onto Santa Rosa Avenue. On the right is another vast expanse of native stone, this one taking up an entire lot next to the house at 576. This massive stone is known locally as Sutcliff Picnic Rock, and used to be a popular destination for climbers and day-trippers. For 20 years or more, though, it has been fenced off and closed to the public, except for special tours arranged by its owners, who bought the rock in order to preserve it as open space and protect it from developers. They live across the street.

Continue along as Santa Rosa crosses Thousand Oaks Boulevard, taking note of the lovely house at 609 and the clipper ship stained glass ornamenting the house at 620. Then, as Santa Rosa meets San Miguel, drop down 10 steps to the lower side of San Miguel and continue straight on. After a bit you'll cross El Paseo Path. Walk on, admiring the fine redwoods on the left, and then turn right onto San Lorenzo. Walk downhill to Colusa, and turn left. Retrace your steps along Colusa, back to Solano, and back to your starting point.

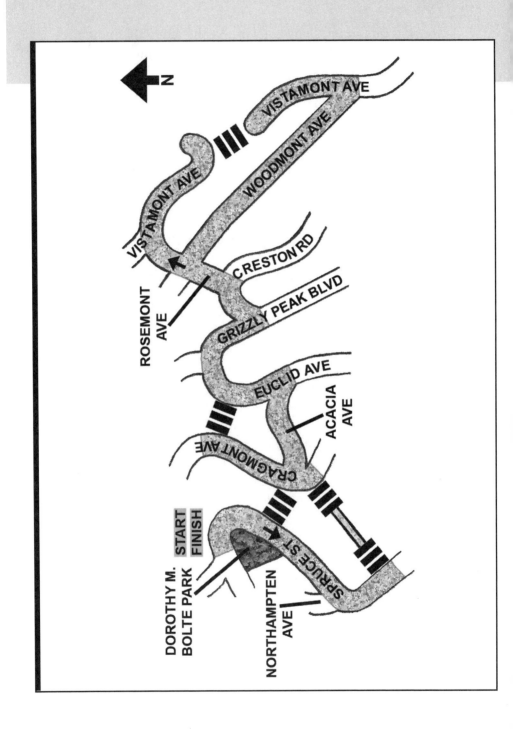

WALK #17

ACACIA WALK
DURATION: **50 minutes**
DISTANCE: **1.8 miles**
STEPS: **208**
DIFFICULTY: **2.5**
BUS: **67**

This relatively short and easy walk is filled with architectural wonders, huge bay views, and a fantastic array of arboreal splendor, and is very suitable for a picnic or lunch-hour walk. It features delightful pathways and great views of Tilden Park.

Begin your walk high up Spruce Avenue, near the corner of Grizzly Peak Boulevard, at charming Dorothy M. Bolte Park—named in memory of a longtime employee of the Berkeley Parks Department. Start by walking downhill from the park, with the big bay views on your right. Ignore Acacia Steps on your left, if you see them. Continue instead past the turning for Northampton Avenue on the right, and just after the house at 619, find the bottom of Acacia Walk.

This is a very narrow and private-looking set of concrete steps, rising close between two houses. Climb up 34 steps, fitted with a nicely-turned wrought iron handrail, to an even narrower pathway that ascends into a low bower. Follow a leaning redwood fence across the leafy walkway as the path widens into good shade along a length of fencing made of stacked firewood. Overhead are tall eucalyptus and cypress trees, as you pass some very quiet backyards. The one on the right sports a modernistic cube of a building. The one on the left sports an earlier idea of modernism—a home clad in asbestos siding.

You emerge, in time, under a gnarled old tree and the remains of a greenhouse or solarium, climbing a final four steps to land at 610 Cragmont Avenue. Turn left and walk up the sidewalk, ignoring once more the Acacia Steps as you pass them on your left. (They come into play later.) Instead, cross the street, and just past the house at 561, find North Path rising on your right.

This is a newer construction of concrete with handrails, the steps sometimes mossy with damp and shade. Climb 70 steps, over multiple landings, stopping halfway up to appreciate the big views behind you. Finish with a final seven steps up to land beside 580 Euclid Avenue.

Cross the street and turn left, heading uphill past the many-windowed newer home at 571, and wind around as Euclid meets Grizzly Peak Boulevard. Bend to the right onto Grizzly Peak, walk to the first corner, then turn left onto Creston Road. Walk a short block, and turn left again onto Rosemont Avenue. Follow Rosemont across Woodmont Avenue, taking note of the Japanese-themed mid-century on the far corner.

Rosemont meets Vistamont. On the corner is a shady yard full of native artistic expressions. Turn right here, and walk straight on, picking up views of Tilden Park below and increasingly massive trees overhead. Admire the street sign for "My Way" and take a moment to ponder Frank Sinatra (who sang the pop song of that name), or Paul Anka (who wrote the song), or the French composers of "Comme d'habitude" (the song on which the song is based). But ignore the many "No Outlet" signs, which serve as a warning to lost motorists, but don't apply to you. Vistamont continues past several more homes and then, just after the house at 616, drops precipitously to the left. Look right to find the top of the marked Vistamont Trail.

This is a narrow trail leading to seven redwood steps down, into a curbed gulley and a broken-concrete walkway rising up the other side. You emerge beside 631 onto a graveled lane. Admire the finely sculpted gardens behind the fence to your left, and the vine-gated and layered hedges to your right.

Take a hard hairpin right turn where Vistamont meets Woodmont once more. Walk along this flat section of heavily shaded roadway—a virtual gallery of architectural delights. Note the Kloss House at 672, with its redwood siding and bright red windows, and the trio of mid-century moderns from designer Roger Lee at 666, 664, and 660. There is a mysterious tree house residence at 640.

The road slopes up, flattens, and begins to fall. As it does, note the impressive Tudor Revival mansion at 605, said to be a 1915 construction from the architectural firm of Ward and Simpson. It is also said that the residence was once owned by the Fogerty family, whose sons John and Tom were among the founding members of Creedence Clearwater Revival.

Walk on as Woodmont meets Rosemont. Turn left. Walk to the corner of Creston and turn right. Turn right again onto Grizzly Peak, and follow this around to the left as the roadway turns into Euclid. Down the hill, past the top of North Steps, and just after the nicely-made clinker-brick-and-beam home at 590, turn right onto Acacia Avenue. A block on, where Acacia meets Cragmont, cross the street and find the top of Acacia Steps.

Descend this handmade pathway of broken concrete pavers—dropping down 86 steps, culminating in some redwood ties—that will deposit you, in time, back on Spruce, across the street from Dorothy M. Bolte Park, and your starting point.

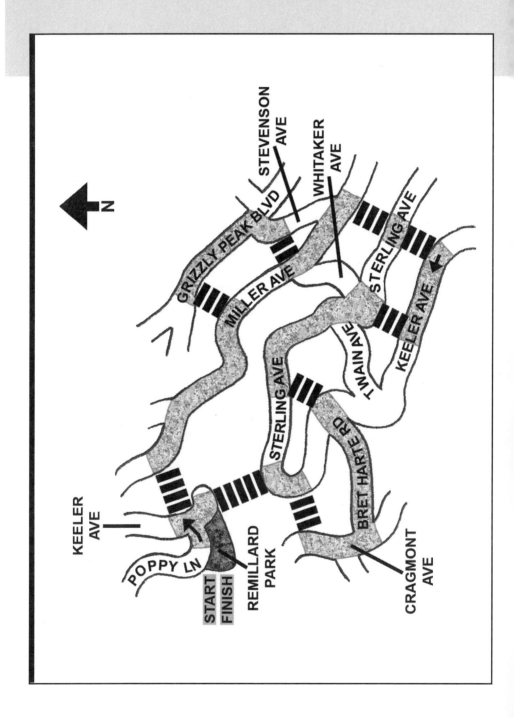

WALK #18

REMILLARD PARK
DURATION: **1 hour, 30 minutes**
DISTANCE: **1.8 miles**
STEPS: **897**
DIFFICULTY: **3.5–4**
BUS: **65, 67**

This is a rigorous walk up and down steep railroad tie path-ways, which are more trails than staircases, with sublime views and possible wildlife sightings.

Begin your walk at Remillard Park, near the corner of Keeler Avenue and Poppy Lane. Acquaint yourself with some local his-tory by reading the plaque attached to the massive ochre stone, behind the split rail fence, that anchors the park to the hillside. Then walk uphill on Poppy, and continue across Keeler onto Poppy Path.

This stairway begins as a wide blacktop driveway rising toward a house painted in startling tones of blue, orange, and red. Close to the house, the driveway becomes redwood steps. Admire the fine collection of hens and roosters, and begin climbing—hard. You'll do 150 steps, plus pathway, without any handrails, to get to the top. Watch for deer or deer tracks.

At the top is a charming brick cottage with a slate roof on Miller Avenue. Turn right, and head uphill, walking past the turning for Latham Lane. The newer, tasteful homes here offer

good views of the bay, if no architectural drama. Just after the
house at 1099, turn left onto the marked section of the steps
known as Bret Harte Lane.

Bret Harte was a California journalist best known for
the colorful short stories *The Luck of Roaring Camp* and *The Outcasts of Poker Flat*. Those stories both appeared in The Overland
Monthly (at times published as *The Californian*, which was at
one point edited by Warren Cheney, developer of Berkeley's
Panoramic area), a San Francisco-based literary magazine that
also drew contributions from East Bay notables like naturalist
John Muir, poet Joaquin Miller, and humorist Ambrose Bierce.

His staircase begins as a redwood tie walkway rising
narrowly between the houses, under a low growth of laurel and
other trees, climbing 84 steps to the top. The stairs deposit
you at 1100 Grizzly Peak Boulevard. Turn right and walk along a
stretch of fairly flat roadway. On a clear day you can see forever,
with bay views, Golden Gate views, and Mount Tamalpais sightings almost guaranteed.

Turn right onto Stevenson Avenue, just before the very
handsome Spanish mansion at 1140 Grizzly Peak. Walk only a
very short distance on Stevenson. As the road bends left, look
on the right for the marked Anne Brower Path.

Named for a popular local woman who was the wife of
noted environmentalist David Brower—you can read all about
him and his rock climbing exploits at Indian Rock Park, part of
Walk #15—this narrow pathway runs closely between two houses, including a striking Cape Cod on the left. The path drops past
big bay views, over 64 steep redwood steps to the street below.

You land at the intersection of Miller and Whitaker Avenue. Turn left and walk along Miller. After a short spell, Stevenson Avenue will angle in on your left. Pass this, but on your
right, just after the house at 1160, find Stevenson Path, beside a
vintage green lamp post.

This top section of Stevenson Path is 142 redwood railroad tie steps, without any handrails, dropping over three seg-
ments, divided by gates. You'll note a couple of signs as you drop

that read, "Public Right of Way. Please Close Gate." You'll note also clumps of rosemary and ceanothus as you pass closely between the houses and their good-looking gardens, decks, and yards.

Descend until the path emerges onto Sterling Avenue. Cross the street and continue down as the second section of Stevenson Path drops 102 redwood steps, without handrails, over multiple landings, culminating in a hairpin turn down to the street. You arrive on Keeler Avenue. Turn right and walk a short distance of this flat street. Just after the house at 1155, find the bottom of mighty Whitaker Path.

Like many of the others in this walk, this is a narrow redwood staircase path, quite steep, and without handrails. It climbs a long 136 steps, past pleasant flower gardens on both sides, up the face of the hillside. Behind you are good views of the city below. Beside you is the suggestion of the presence of deer: Young fruit trees and shrubs are in wooden cages.

At the top, you arrive on Sterling Avenue. Bear left and walk along, past the turning on the left for Twain Avenue. Shortly after, you will come upon a wild architectural expression of Googie-style modernism on the left—a hillside home for *The Jetsons* that, at the time of this writing, looked abandoned. Walk on, past less startling homes, between which are good bay views. Then, just after the house at 1084, look for Bret Harte Path on your left.

This is another sharp descent of 79 redwood steps running past a profusion of wild berries growing under deep shade, which culminates in a concrete staircase of 35 steps. You are deposited onto another section of Keeler. Walk to the right, but only for a moment, then catch the left downhill onto Bret Harte Road.

Descend a long block, observing the delightful dell on your right, with its crisscrossing bridges and pathways, and admiring the enchanted entrance to the house at 131, which features an attractive wooden bridge to the front yard. Turn right at the first opportunity onto Cragmont Avenue. Walk straight on, ignoring the turning for the continuation of Bret Harte Road, and then quite soon find the bottom of Sterling Path on your right.

This begins as a wide concrete staircase, rising 14 steps into a narrow dirt pathway. This is followed by a series of 34 redwood steps, past the gate for a handsome house half-hidden on the right, and an uneven concrete staircase of 45 more steps. Climb past an overgrowth of wild berries and Spanish broom, to land once more on Sterling. Turn left and walk across the driveways for both 1070 and 1064. Just after the second driveway, not 50 feet from the top of Sterling Path, find tiny Keeler Path on the left.

This is a very narrow dirt trail, running through the houses, bordered on the left side by a wall of bamboo. The pathway drops downhill slightly and carries you under the limbo-low limbs of an elderly bay laurel tree. Enjoy a shady stretch of path, and a riot of wild berry bushes and bay laurel trees, to culminate in 12 redwood tie stairs rising up to Keeler Avenue. Admire the magnificent gardens on your right, which belong to 1045 Keeler, and the towering eucalyptus trees on your left, which belong to Remillard Park. Dead ahead is Poppy Lane, and your starting point.

Overleaf: Lake Merritt and the Oakland skyline.

PART THREE

OAKLAND: THE SOUTH AND EAST

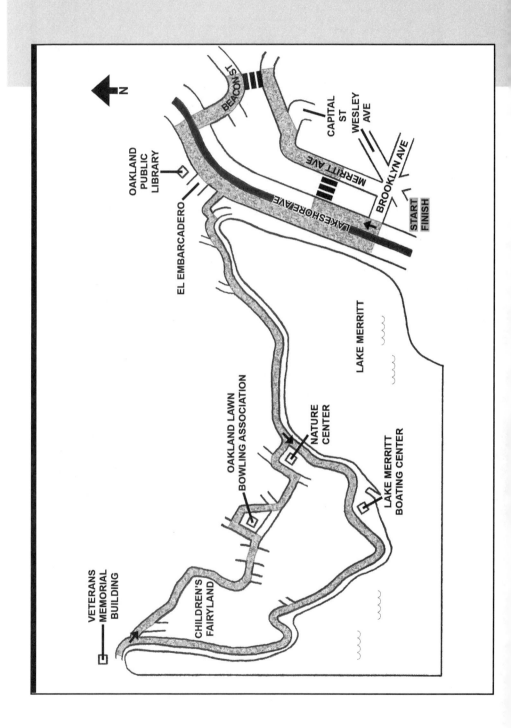

WALK #19

LAKE MERRITT CASCADES
DURATION: **1 hour, 15 minutes**
DISTANCE: **3 miles**
STEPS: **206**
DIFFICULTY: **2.5**
BUS: **26, 57, 653, 657**

Here is a walk that's long on distance and short on steps, but offers an unparalleled excursion around the northern end of Lake Merritt and that neighborhood's delights. Combined with a visit to the Saturday farmer's market, it's a great way to start your weekend. Birders should bring their bird books and binoculars.

Begin this walk on the eastern side of Lake Merritt, near the corner of Lakeshore and Brooklyn Avenues, perhaps with a coffee from the nearby Haddon Hill Café, at 504 Wesley Avenue, two blocks east of the lake. It's a Four Barrel Coffee dispensary, and they pull a powerful espresso.

Find your way to the lakeside, and begin walking north along the water, keeping to the eastern side of Lakeshore Avenue. (Use the historic Grand Lake Theater as a landmark, if you don't know your north from your south, and head for that. The eastern side of the avenue is the one *away* from the lakeside.) After a block's length, just after the building at 2250, you'll find your first staircase on the right.

You may see the hardbodies first. This is Cleveland Cascade, and it attracts a large contingent of physical fitness enthusiasts, who on the weekend can be seen stretching, flexing, grunting, and gasping their way up and down the lovely double-barrelled staircase. Ignore them, if you can, and as you begin to climb imagine instead a fine cascading waterfall coming directly down the center of this historic staircase. That's what it offered in its infancy. Now, the central cascade area is nicely landscaped with plants.

Climb 17 steps up to the first level, then 43 to the next, then a final 67 up to the top, and nine more to the street. The intermediary levels are fitted with benches, and the whole structure is framed and shaded by redwoods, oaks, and sweet pittosporum. These somewhat obscure the view of the lake, but better views are to come.

At the top, past another knot of exercise nuts, hang a left and walk uphill on Merritt Avenue. Here you will find overbearing apartment blocks, offering fine peeks at the view between them. On a clear day, you can see Mount Tamalpais, in bits and pieces. You also get a nice perspective on the gorgeous brick confection that is the Bellevue Staten Apartments, a beautiful 1929 building from the hand of San Francisco commercial designer Herman Carl Baumann. Nearer to hand, notice the nice tile work around the doorway at 493 as you pass.

Continue past the turning for Capital Street, marked by a handsome traffic circle, staying to the left on Merritt. Then, just after the building at 563, and before you meet Wesley Avenue, find your second staircase, marked at the top by a thick, low-growing Washington palm. This is a fall of 79 steps, quite steep and narrow as it nears the bottom, split by a sturdy metal handrail, that takes you down to Beacon Street. Turn left and walk downhill, passing Boden Street on the left and running straight into Lake Shore.

Cross this busy boulevard at the crosswalk, and then turn left. Walk past the lakeside branch of the Oakland Public Library—which maintains a public restroom—cross El Embarcadero, and walk toward the lakefront itself. Aim for the big wide columns that frame a gateway to the water.

The area before you used to be an open wetlands, a tidal

basin that drained into Oakland harbor and, because of this natural flushing, was the city's principal sewer. A scheme to tame the wetlands was organized by Dr. Samuel Merritt, a successful local physician, lakefront property owner, and the thirteenth mayor of the City of Oakland. Merritt organized funds to build a dam, dredge the wetlands, and turn them into a lake, which was duly named in his honor.

When you've entered the Lake Merritt gates, turn right onto the pathway that fronts the water and begin a partial circumnavigation. Admire the fine old street lamps as you go, which eventually will be joined by smaller lights that make up what locals call the "Necklace of Lights" around this section of the lake—something of an eyesore during the day, but very pretty at night.

A nice long flat walk follows, past 10,000 pigeons and an equal number of Canada geese, whose defecatory habits have made them rather unpopular with locals—especially dog owners, since protecting these "migratory" birds, who no longer migrate but have made the lake their permanent home, means keeping all canines out of the park.

In time, you'll come to a totem pole and a lakeside nature center, said to contain its own live beehive. Bear left here, continuing your counterclockwise journey around the water. You'll note cages and enclosures for fowl of some kind, and the Lake Merritt Boating Center, where boats can be rented. Keep this building on your left to maintain steady on the lakefront path, which in time will become a dirt trail to the left of the paved walkway. The trail dips down, under some fine low-growing oaks, across a small beach, and past a dinosaur-bones play area.

As you continue around the lake, to your left will appear the relatively new Cathedral of Christ the Light, the seat of the Archdiocese of Oakland, and the home of the city's Bishop. (The city's very first bishop is buried here.) Opened in 2008, the remarkable building is the design of San Francisco architect Craig W. Hartman, who likened the experience of standing inside his steel-glass-wood creation to the experience of standing in "a canopy of tall redwood trees in a wooded glade."

Just ahead, of more ancient vintage, is the stately Veterans Memorial Building. Erected in 1930, it features lovely arched windows and, inside, a basketball court. In the 1960s it was host to rock shows, including some by the Grateful Dead. It's now a senior center, perhaps serving the same audience it did 40 years ago.

Here at the top of the lake, you may choose to continue around. The entire circumnavigation is approximately a 3.5 mile commitment. That's for a different day. For now, turn and follow the path back as it doglegs off to the right and rises away from the lake, up a slight hill and behind the Children's Fairyland sign. Where the pathway makes a "V," bear left, passing in front of the Fairyland. Dating from the early 1950s, this is said to be America's very first theme park, and to have been a model for Walt Disney when he was planning his own Southern California playground. It is a favorite of local children, and off-limits to adults arriving without any.

Bear left past Fairyland, crossing a wide lawn and aiming for a low, adobe-style building with a red tile roof. This is the home of the Oakland Lawn Bowling Association, a venerable institution, almost 100 years old, whose finely textured bowling pitches are to your right and left. Admire the delicate mosaic tile portraits of bowlers in action, dating from 1912, then turn left and walk around behind the building. Here you will find more lawns, sometimes in use as croquet fields by people who take their croquet very, very seriously.

Continue straight on, under some oaks, across a pathway, heading toward the nature center and its totem pole. Veer to the left of this, perhaps taking advantage of its public restrooms, and return to the lakeside path. Here are up-close views of some of the fine old lakeside architecture.

As you return to the lakeside and look south across the water, you can also see a very large, stark, white building. That's the Alameda County Court building. At the lake's edge is the relatively new "Gondola Servizio," where you can have the

Venetian experience, complete with Italian-warbling gondo-lier, for $75 an hour. To its left, lying low in the water, is the old Lake Merritt boathouse, now a restaurant known as Lake Cha-let Seafood Bar and Grill. The original building was designed in 1909 by Berkeley's John Galen Howard—as a pump house for Oakland's fire department. Behind that, the large white Mission Revival building is the Islamic Center of Northern California. It was originally a Scottish Rite Temple, built in 1908. You may also be able to see the charming Tribune Tower, lighted at night with the newspaper's name. Since 2007, the building has housed only offices and condos.

In time you will return to the gateway. If it's a Saturday morning and you're in the mood, turn left here, cross El Embarcadero, walk under the freeway on Lakeshore, and turn left into the farmer's market. You could also get in a little extra exercise by leaving the lakeside and crossing Lakeshore at the next pathway, walking up Boden to Beacon, and climbing the steps to Merritt. From there, turn right, follow Merritt up and over the crest, and catch the Cleveland Cascade coming back down.

If it's not a Saturday, or you're not in the mood, continue around the lake, enjoying increasingly better views of the water and the far shores. When you come to the first stop light, you have come to Brooklyn, and your starting point.

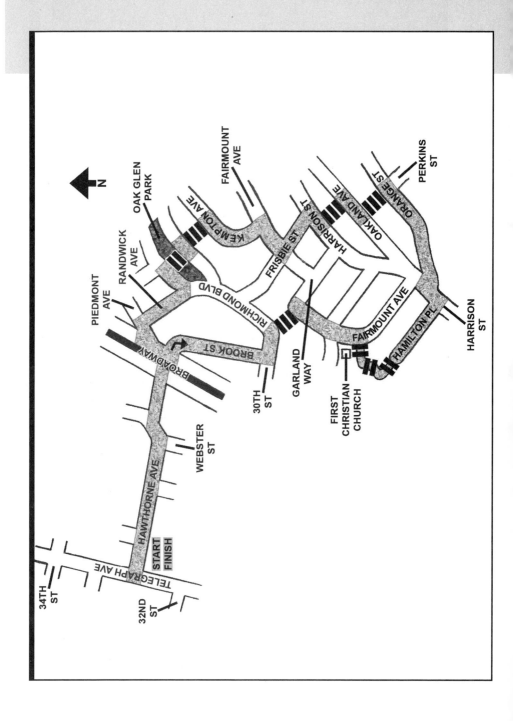

WALK #20

BROADWAY AND OAK GLEN PARK
DURATION: **1 hour**
DISTANCE: **2.5 miles**
STEPS: **370**
DIFFICULTY: **2.5–3**
BUS: **1,800**

Here is a relatively flat walk along some charming old streets, past some charming old houses, through one of Oakland's oldest neighborhoods.

Start your walk on Telegraph Avenue, near the intersection of Hawthorne Avenue, perhaps with a glass of something refreshing at the Commonwealth Café at the corner of 29th or a bakery snack from the immense and venerable A Taste of Denmark Bakery at the corner of 34th. When you are fortified, leave Telegraph going east on Hawthorne, heading for Pill Hill.

This used to be hospital central, and it's still dominated by medical buildings. On your right, as the road begins to rise, is Providence Hospital. (Behind it is Kaiser Permanente.) Further on, as you reach the summit at Summit Street, is Alta Bates Summit Medical Center.

Once over the top, bear left at Webster Street, then turn right immediately to continue down the hill on Hawthorne, with another medical building to your left and the glass block wall of a very old car dealership to your right. At the corner, use the crosswalk to cross Broadway. Then continue straight ahead, more or less, onto Brook Street.

The busy road behind you is the Auto Row section of Broadway. Just as hospitals proliferated on Pill Hill, so here the dealerships and their satellite businesses have spread. As you walk along, you'll find some sturdy older houses on the left and a raft of auto body, upholstery, electrical, and repair shops on the right. Where Brook meets 30th Street, turn left. Walk half a block and you will find your first staircase.

It comes with a charming surprise. A block from Auto Row is a little creek, cloaked in bushes and shrubs, with a little wooden footbridge over it. Cross the bridge, then climb 52 steps, helped by a handrail. Until recently, the staircase was host to a "Space Invader" tile logo—perhaps the work of the Paris street artist whose mosaic tiles began decorating Paris in the 1990s. After recent staircase improvements here, however, the tile disappeared.

At the top, you find yourself at the corner of Fairmount Avenue and Garland Way. Turn right and head downhill on Fairmount. Cross 29th Street, staying on Fairmont, and walk past the striking First Christian Church, a 1928 structure with a magnificent doorway and tiled dome.

Enter the church parking lot, just after the church building, and walk straight on, keeping to the left side of the lot. At the far end, under a spreading oak tree, find your next staircase. It begins in wood, dropping down 41 shady steps, then gives way to a concrete walkway. This shifts and turns, and brings you to a relative oddity: a staircase intersection. Turn left and climb 71 concrete steps, fitted with a sturdy railing, up to the cul-de-sac end of Hamilton Place. Many of the old homes here have stood since the early 1900s with very little "improvement." Walk downhill, admiring the Victorian and Craftsman touches, until you hit Harrison Street.

Cross Harrison, using the crosswalk, then turn left. At the first opportunity, bear right onto Orange Street and begin a slight climb. Here, too, are some handsome old homes, including a finely-adorned Victorian at 182 and a sort of Prairie Revival shingled home at 201. As the road rises, Perkins Street comes in on the right. At the same time, after the large stucco house at 243, find Perkins Way on your left.

This passage begins as a wide sloping sidewalk, then drops down to conclude with 19 steps under a heavily-beamed wooden overhang supported by clinker brick columns. You're on Oakland Avenue now. Cross carefully, using the crosswalk, then turn right, walking past two little storefront businesses. Just after them, find tiny Frisbie Way on your left.

This is a narrow walkway with 14 steps down and a slope of sidewalk that drops you back on Harrison once more. Turn right and walk to the first corner, where Harrison meets Frisbie. Cross Harrison carefully, in the crosswalk, and walk up a steep block of Frisbie. Then take the first right turning, back onto Fairmount, past a trio of handsome palm trees. Turn left at the first corner, onto Kempton Avenue, and climb a bit more.

On your left is the pocket park known as Oak Park, fitted with a children's play area and some benches, and presided over by another grand palm. Walk past this and follow Kempton as it bends to the right and enters deep shade and a lane of larger, older homes. Between the houses at 3287 and 3301 you'll find your next staircase. This is a big one, starting as a short walkway and turning quickly into a deeply shaded group of 159 wide concrete steps, split by a handrail, over multiple landings.

You land on Richmond Boulevard, across the street from charming Oak Glen Park. Walk straight ahead, into the park, and cross the creek on the stone footbridge under heavy oak shade. Climb 14 steps, on the other side, to street level, and turn left onto the other side of Richmond. Walk along the park to the first corner, and turn right onto Randwick Avenue. Straight ahead, you will find yourself on Piedmont, fronting Broadway and Auto Row once more.

Turn left. Piedmont merges into Broadway. Cross with the light at Hawthorne and walk up the slight rise, past the car dealership with the glass block wall, bearing left at Webster and right back onto Hawthorne, up and over the top of Pill Hill. Follow Hawthorne to Telegraph, and your starting point.

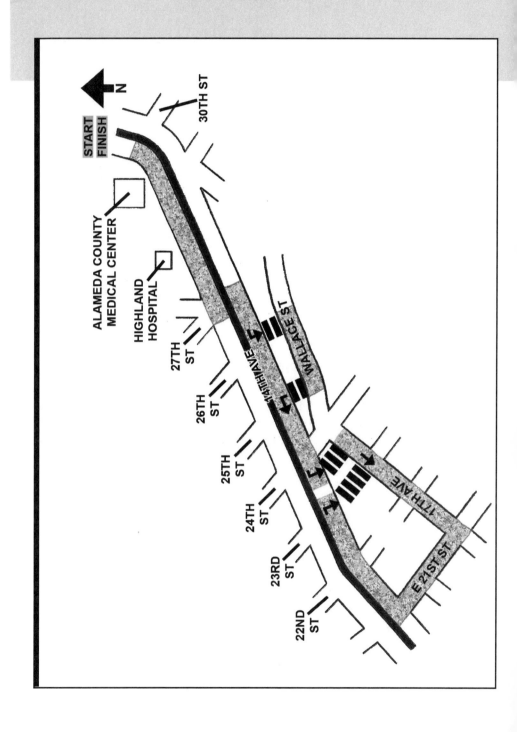

WALK #21

HIGHLAND HOSPITAL
DURATION: **1 hour**
DISTANCE: **2 miles**
STEPS: **268**
DIFFICULTY: **3**
BUS: **11, 653, 657, 658, 680, 805**

This is an urban walk through one of Oakland's oldest neighborhoods. It begins beside a historic hospital, and includes charming walk-streets. Graffiti and broken bottles suggest it might not be a great place to walk at night.

Begin this walk on 14th Avenue, near E. 30th Street—just south of the 580 freeway. Walk south, or downhill, on 14th, as the massive Alameda County Medical Center rises on your right.

As you approach the corner of 27th Street, note that the character of the architecture has changed. Just past the new medical center is old Highland Hospital. Built in 1927 on a hilltop, it's a fantastic example of California Spanish Baroque architecture. The closest things I know to it are Oakland's First Christian Church on Fairmont, a 1928 work by William Weeks, and San Francisco's magnificent Mission High School building, next to Dolores Park.

Stop at the corner and turn around to get a feeling for the grandeur of this historic structure. Through two massive gates are a wide lawn and a flagpole, where a faded Stars and Stripes still waves. Two huge staircases, fed by underground passages, carry patients and staff uphill to this majestic building.

This side of the structure is usually closed, but on week-days you can enter the gates on the left and walk up the driveway to get a feel for the facility. Don't say I told you so, but if the Staff Entrance doors are open, you can wander through the hospital halls, which felt entirely haunted to me....

Returning to our walk, cross 14th at 27th to the east (or left) side of the street, and continue walking downhill, past a line of cute shingled bungalows. When you come to the sign for E. 26th Street, stop. Look to the left and find your first staircase.

This begins as a sloping sidewalk between two graffitied fences, then becomes a wide concrete staircase split by a steel handrail. It rises 61 steps to deposit you on Wallace Street, under the cover of oak and eucalyptus trees. Turn right and head downhill, past modest old cottages on the right and a hillside in great need of a garbage truck on the left. Note the manhole covers marked as the work of Phoenix Iron Works, Oakland, a local foundry dating from 1901 that crafted a high percentage of the manhole covers and street drains for the area.

Walk on, but not far. Just after the guard-dog Doberman and the four pea-green garages on your right, find the next stair-case. This is E. 25th Street, a staircase recently restored, with new handrails and 13 steps dropping down onto a wide concrete sidewalk. When you land again on 14th Avenue, turn left, and head downhill. You'll pass a line of old clapboard houses, many of them in original, unrestored condition—note the tiny, narrow garages on the ground floor, perfect for a 1920s Model T, not so good for anything built after that.

Cross E. 24th Street in the crosswalk, past a knot of ancient, suffering palm trees. Admire the matched-set frame houses at 2346 and 2342. Then, look quick: On the left is Comstock Way, your next staircase.

Like its nearby fellows, this begins as a sloping walkway and turns into a wide set of stairs, split by a metal handrail. But unlike the others, this is a real live walk-street—the house on your right probably has no other way in and out of the front door except the staircase. Climb up 52 stairs, a little uneven but fairly clean, to land on 17th Avenue. Cross the street, and turn right.

At the corner, do not fail to appreciate the lovely, mostly unrestored Victorian corner house, with the conical roof, at 2302.

Walk straight on, across E. 23rd and E. 22nd, noting the handsome old frame houses at 2230, 2222, and 2214, as well as the big brown job at 2142—once majestic, with a sad, added-on porch sagging off its back side.

You pick up interesting bay views off to the right as 17th begins to descend. Drop down to E. 21st Street, take a right, and enjoy an architectural oddity. All of the houses on your right, 10 or 12 of them in a row, were built from the same set of plans. Note the strangely angled columns, mirrored from one bungalow to the next. For an alternative, check out the fine looking Queen Anne, with the porch curving around two sides of it, across the street at 1605.

Turn right at the bottom of the hill, back onto 14th Avenue. Walk up past E. 21st and E. 22nd, appreciating as you go some more of those strangely angled columns. Was there a fire sale on these things? They're everywhere!

Where you come to a sign for E. 23rd Street, stop and look to the right. Here is your final staircase up. Saving the best for last, it's a big one—starting as a sloped walkway, marked by a contractor's stamp reading "Tribuzio Bros. Oakland 1925," and turning into a wide staircase divided by a steel handrail. It climbs a very symmetrical 90 steps—seven sets of 10, one set of 20—and like its predecessor is a real walk-street. There is no other way in or out of the little bungalows you pass as you climb up.

You land at the corner of 17th Avenue and E. 23rd Street. Across the street is that handsome Victorian you passed a while back. Turn left this time, though, and walk north on 17th. There are good views here of Highland Hospital, its mosaic tiled turrets rising high above the tree line.

Don't walk far. Just after the house at 2315, at the top of Comstock Way, turn left and drop back down the 52 stairs. When you hit 14th, turn right and retrace your steps uphill. Appreciate as you go the creative use of tile on the side of 2534. Cross 14th again at E. 27th to get a final good look at Highland Hospital. Once past it, you arrive back at E. 30th, and your starting point.

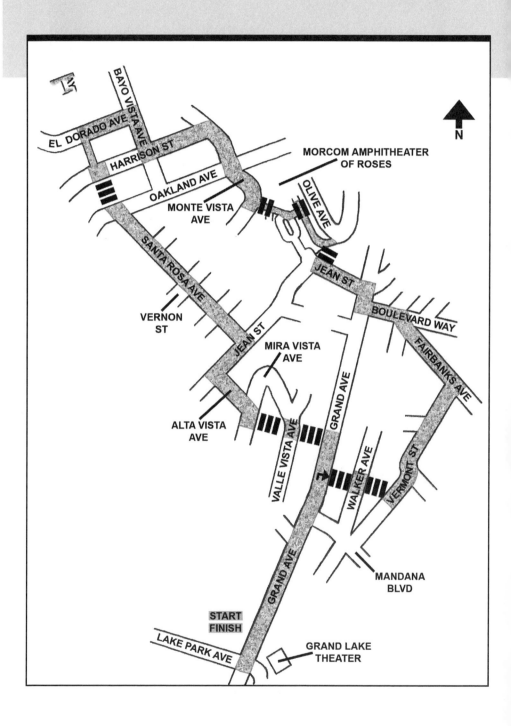

WALK #22

GRAND LAKE'S ROSE GARDEN
DURATION: **1 hour, 15 minutes**
DISTANCE: **2.4 miles**
STEPS: **461**
DIFFICULTY: **3**
BUS: **12, 57, 653, 657, 658, 688, B**

This moderately flat walk, loaded with hidden staircases and walkways, is anchored by a visit to an impressive rose garden. Along the way are some marvelous mountain views.

Begin this Oakland walk somewhere near the intersection of Grand Avenue and Lake Park Avenue, perhaps with a double bill at the historic Grand Lake picture palace, or a coffee at The Coffee Mill, which boasts of being "Oakland's Oldest Coffee House," or a cocktail at any of several bars and lounges on Grand, among them the alluringly divey Smitty's, The Alley, or The Libertine.

After you've sucked up whatever beverage you like, begin walking north on Grand, with the movie theater and the freeway at your back, on the east (or right) side of the street. Just past Mandana Boulevard, beyond the 7-Eleven and the Cycle Sports and chiropractor's office at 3540, find your first staircase.

This is Davidson Way, which starts as a sloping sidewalk shaded by eucalyptus and pyracantha and concludes with a railed staircase rising up 71 wide, shallow steps. You land on

Walker Avenue. Cross Walker as the staircase continues dead
ahead, losing its handrail, becoming steeper, and turning quite
uneven. Take care, as the upper half of Davidson Way climbs un-
steadily up another 156 steps, between two low mossy walls.

At the top, turn left onto Vermont Street, continuing to
climb as the road meets Prince Street on the right. Stay to the
left as Vermont bends and flat-
tens. At the corner, you will
be treated to a fine view of the
Oakland hills, including the
deep green lawns of Mountain
View Cemetery.

Follow Vermont as it be-
gins to descend, past the elderly
block house at 863 and its as-
bestos-sided neighbor at 865.
Vermont bellies out at Weldon
Avenue, then climbs again. Follow this, past the deep red Lincoln Log home at 990, and then
turn left as Vermont "Ts" into
Fairbanks Avenue.

Fairbanks drops sharp-
ly, giving up all the altitude
you gained on Davidson Way,
to land at a complicated intersection where Fairbanks meets
Boulevard Way, Sylvan Way, and
Walker Avenue. Walk straight
ahead, to the degree that is possible, following Boulevard until you hit Grand Avenue once
more. Turn right at Grand, past
the corner liquor store with the

SECRET PATH THROUGH
THE REDWOOD SHADE.

great tiles set in brick over the door. At the first opportunity, cross Grand with the light, at Jean Street.

Walk straight up Jean, appreciating the strange artistic expressions in stone on your left—stone walls, stone cacti, stone birds and ducks. Continue up Jean. Ahead of you is the Morcom Amphitheater of Roses, fronted by a collection of impressive

Greek columns. Just before these, and the entrance to the rose garden itself, find the next staircase to the right side of the roadway.

Climb 83 somewhat uneven steps, keeping the oaks and redwoods of the park on your left and the pretty bungalow apartments on your right. At the top of the staircase, where the park ends and Olive Avenue begins, make a dogleg left and catch the asphalt walkway going back down into the park. This will drop down to another set of stairs. Take these 18 steps down to a lovely oval pond, framed in roses, to the center of the flower garden. The park itself was built as a Works Progress Administration project in 1932, and, like Lake Merritt, was named after a former Oakland mayor. Admission is free, and the park is open daily from dawn to dusk.

Bear right, walking around the top of the pond. Enjoy the roses. Then take the very wide rose-colored stairs, split by a metal handrail, climbing up the top of the park. Walk 102 steps up, to land at the edge of the park at the corner of Monte Vista Avenue and Vernon Street.

After a backward glance at the arrangement of roses below, walk straight ahead and up a short stretch of Monte Vista. At the first corner, cross busy Oakland Avenue and continue on Monte Vista, past the large Plymouth United Church of Christ and, next door, a noble old home in need of restoration.

Turn left at the first corner onto Harrison Street, enjoying some big historic homes. (I liked the wide porch at 3932 and the comically conical roof and circular doorway at 3912.) At the first corner, where you meet the restored, historic Locke House—a John Hudson Thomas design from 1911—turn right onto Bayo Vista Avenue. Walk a block, past one more faded beauty at 103, and turn left onto El Dorado Avenue.

The homes here are in considerably better repair, and are shaded by a row of large liquidambar trees. Walk along, but keep a sharp eye out. Just after the house at 602, find tiny Oscar's Alley on your left.

This narrow sidewalk rises slightly past a pair of

clapboard homes on the left and a redwood fence on the right. It meets another stretch of Harrison, and then continues across the street after a slight jog to the left. Take nine steps up, onto a sloping sidewalk, and climb this until you emerge on Oakland Avenue by the corner of Santa Rosa Avenue.

Cross the street and aim for Santa Rosa, but pause for a moment to appreciate some local architecture. Behind you, across Oakland, is a brick and stucco monument of Towne House at 629 (once a fine private home, but for many decades a Bay Area Community Services mental health facility). Closer to you, opposite Towne House, is a low-roofed, slap-sided Craftsman, in deep browns, at 610.

When you're done comparing houses, walk down Santa Rosa as it descends slightly, passing Mariposa and Vernon, and rises again to pass Chetwood Street and then to end in a "T" intersection at Jean. Turn right onto Jean. After a short block, turn left on Alta Vista Avenue, and after another short block, turn right onto Mira Vista Avenue. Then, on your left, between the houses at 540 and 538, find your final staircase, Bonham Way.

Descend three steps and walk along a sloping sidewalk, under heavy oak and pine shadows. Pass a tree house, a redwood hot tub, and other backyard detritus, then drop down 19 more steps to land on Valle Vista Avenue. Cross the street and continue as the sloping walkway slopes down a bit more. You emerge on busy Grand Avenue. Turn right, heading downhill, and find your way back to your starting point.

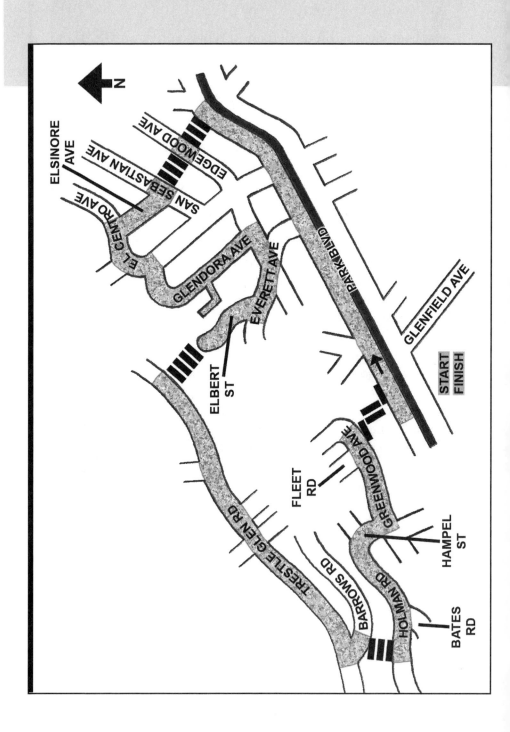

WALK #23

GLENVIEW
DURATION: **1 hour**
DISTANCE: **2.2 miles**
STEPS: **206**
DIFFICULTY: **2**
BUS: **18, 618**

This is a charming walk through some house-proud neigh-borhoods lined with sycamore and plane trees—a good shady stroll for a hot afternoon.

Begin this walk on Park Boulevard near the corner of Glen-field Avenue, in the heart of the tiny Glenview commercial dis-trict, perhaps with lunch at The Blackberry Bistro or a coffee from Ultimate Grounds. When you've supped, walk north on Park, toward the hills.

Walk up this divided boulevard that once had a streetcar running up its spine, past some attractive stucco bungalows in the Craftsman style, and some nice wooden buildings like the one marked by big palms at 4425. Cross Wellington, Everett, and El Centro. Then, just before Park widens further, catch El-sinore Walk on your left, just after the house at 4645.

This path is a narrow walkway, nicely landscaped, pass-ing between the houses. It will take you across to Edgewood, across the street, then up three stairs and down nine, to con-tinue to San Sebastian Avenue. Cross the street and continue straight ahead, down what is now Elsinore Avenue.

This will drop sharply, past some appealing small hous-es of older vintage than those on Park. As the hill steepens, turn left onto El Centro and continue downhill. As El Centro bends hard to the left, you bend to the right onto Glendora Avenue.

This climbs and bends, too, then flattens out, past some very handsome shingle-sided homes, like those at 1015 and 1031. Between 1031 and 1043 you can get sneaky peeks of downtown Oakland. Just past the house at 1075, you'll find the marked Glendora Path on your right.

This is an anomaly—a public walkway that appears on maps to connect you to a cul-de-sac street below but which, in fact, does *not* connect to anything at all. I have my suspicions that it once ran clear through, and has since been gated by local residents. I could be wrong. It's a charming little sidewalk on the back side of some houses, and offers a back yard view of a couple of very good back yard farming ventures. One house on the right, as you turn the corner in the pathway, has bee boxes; the one next door has a marvelous garden—almost a farm—with enough vegetables to feed a small village.

But the path ends. Turn around, return to Glendora Avenue, and turn right. Walk to the corner and turn right onto Edgewood Avenue. Walk again to the next corner, and turn right again onto Everett. After a short distance turn right onto Elbert Street. Walk downhill, and find the cul-de-sac where the inter-rupted walkway, I believe, once landed. Exploring here is not recommended.

Suddenly, it seems, you are in the countryside. Here are big old homes surrounded by big old trees. Nothing has changed here in 80 years but the automobiles. It's difficult to imagine that busy Park Avenue is only blocks away.

Straight ahead, to the left of the garage attached to the faded Craftsman at 1000, you'll see a length of sidewalk. Walk along this, into the deep shade, and find your next staircase. This one is a beautiful curved structure with a handrail, drop-ping down an elegant 43 steps onto a pathway, which turns right and runs narrowly between redwood fences to deposit you on the upper reaches of Trestle Glen Road.

Take a left, and begin a stroll through a classic East Bay neighborhood. On weekend afternoons the yards are full of kids playing and parents trimming trees and mowing lawns. The houses are well-tended and offer the occasional creative expression—like the conical witch-hat turrets at 1575 and 1569, and the profusion of leaded glass at 1544.

Pass Humphrey Place, Norwood Avenue, and Creed Road. Then, when Trestle Glen bends to the right, turn left onto Barrows Road. After a very short stretch, you'll find your next staircase on the right, just after the house at 1329. This one is again a concrete set of stairs fitted with handrails, rising under a heavy canopy of pyracantha or cotoneaster bushes. (I can never remember which is which, but they have loads of red berries.) It climbs 36 steps onto a sloping walkway, passing under some rather low-growing trees and shrubs, and continues another 43 steps up to land on Holman Road.

Turn left, and walk uphill on Holman, toward some high-tension power lines squeezed in tight between two houses. Walk past the turning for Bates Road, as Holman begins to slope downhill and bend right. Follow the bend, and turn uphill for a steep stretch of Hampel Street. At the crest, turn left from Hampel onto Greenwood Avenue.

Walk on, for a long block, until just after Fleet Road comes in on the left. On the right, just after the house at 4168, find your final staircase. (Architecture buffs may walk on slightly and gander at the building at 4182.)

Turn right, up the stairs, and climb—you're almost done. This structure, marked at both ends with a contractor's stamp reading "J.H. Fitzmaurice, Oakland, Union Made Local 584," climbs 15 steps onto a sloping walkway, turns left and right again, then rises 69 steps over multiple landings.

You land on Park Avenue, just in front of a handsome set of storefronts containing a shoe repair shop and a lock and key shop. Turn left and walk past these, uphill a block, to Glenfield and your starting point.

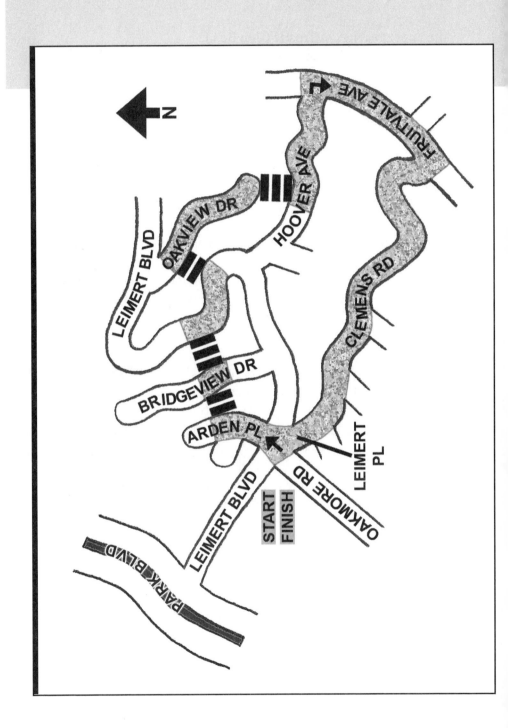

WALK #24

OAKMORE
DURATION: **30 minutes**
DISTANCE: **1.2 miles**
STEPS: **337**
DIFFICULTY: **3–3.5**
BUS: **18, 618, 688**

Here is a short but charming walk, with steep staircases and towering views of the southern Oakland area. For extra length, pair this one with Walk #25, Trestle Glen and Piedmont, or Walk #23, Glenview.

Begin this walk in Oakmore, near the intersection of Park Boulevard and Leimert Boulevard, in the little commercial district where Leimert meets Oakmore Road. (Leimert is named after the developer of the historic Lakeshore Highlands residential area.) Have a snack from old-timey Rocky's Market, or a slice from Red Boy Pizza. Then set out, heading north on tiny Arden Place. After the house at 4326, find the nicely-signposted "City of Oakland Public Stairway" on the right. This is Bridgeview Path.

A short walkway leads to a wide concrete staircase, framed in dark green handrails, that rises 48 steps to land on Bridgeview Drive. Cross the road and, between more dark handrails, find the next set of stairs—an increasingly steep set of stairs, again between dark green handrails and past a fine big redwood, going up a sharp 113 steps to land on another stretch of Leimert.

Turn right, heading slightly downhill as the road bends and falls, catching nice views of Oakland on the right side. Note the prevalence here of stamps in the sidewalk left by the concrete contractors who poured them—V. Dizillo of Oakland left his mark in 1933, as did Ed Doty in 1940, and Lovisone in 1938. Proud craftsman these were!

Cross the street. On the left side, after a short spell and just past the house at 1745, find the next staircase—again marked as a public stairway, but this time made of *wood.* These climb a dramatic 111 steps, each one a thunky wooden footfall. Halfway up are very big views of the Port of Oakland, Oakland International Airport, and the southern end of the bay. On clear days you can see as far south as the San Mateo Bridge.

You're now on Oakview Drive. Turn right, and walk flat along this pleasant street as it begins to bend and rise. (Note some more contractors' stamps. A. MacDonald worked here in 1933.) Then, just before the road turns left and abruptly ends, after the house at 1989, find the next staircase—going *down* this time, on the right.

This set is marked with some other concrete stamps, very historical ones. They read, "W.P.A. 1939," a marker indicating the work of the Depression-era Works Projects Administration, Franklin Delano Roosevelt's far-reaching New Deal effort to use unemployed American crafts workers to build or repair the country's roads, bridges, public buildings, and even staircases. This one begins with a drop of 23 steps onto a sloping sidewalk, and ends with a drop of a final 42, to deposit you at 1950 Hoover Avenue.

Turn left on Hoover and walk along, noting the fine old oaks and the twin chalet-style homes at 1962 and 1968. (One of my walking friends referred to them as "Tudor-Lite.") The road is newer here, as indicated by some more contractors' stamps. See the work of R. C. Wolfe, from 1954 and 1955, near the property lines on the sidewalk in front of the house at 2037.

Hawks sometimes twirl above you—perhaps visiting

from nearby Sequoia Lodge Park—as the road rises to meet Fruitvale Avenue. Turn right and head downhill, pausing to admire the cupola-cornered confection on the left at 4300—a 4,000 square-foot mansion said to have been built in 1883. It has a fine wide porch, and fine bay views, and must once have stood all by itself on this hill.

Fruitvale begins to descend sharply. Where it meets Clemens Road, turn hard right and follow Clemens as it bends and follows the hillside around. Note the terraced gardens on the right-hand side, the below-street-level foundations and garages on the left, and the fine oak and cypress trees in front of the house at 1939 and the strangely barricaded fortress next door.

Cross Lyman Road and Waterhouse Road, then veer right and slightly uphill onto Leimert Place. This will rise a short block and return you to Leimert Boulevard, and your starting point.

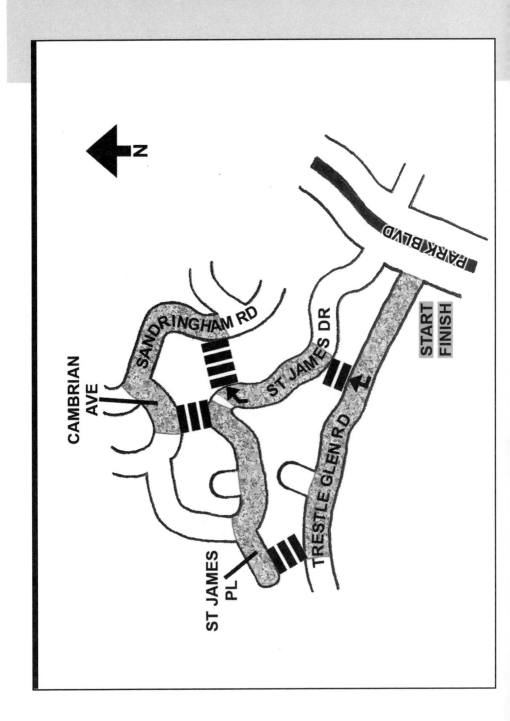

WALK #25

TRESTLE GLEN AND PIEDMONT
DURATION: **45 minutes**
DISTANCE: **1.4 miles**
STEPS: **370**
DIFFICULTY: **3**
BUS: **18, 618, 688**

This is a short, sweet walk that includes perhaps the best-looking and best-maintained staircases in the entire Bay Area. For a more strenuous workout, do it backwards, or go to the bottom of the final staircase and return the way you came.

Begin this walk on the border of Oakland and Piedmont, near the intersection of Park Boulevard and Trestle Glen Road, in the shadow of Corpus Christ Catholic Church. Note before you leave the vast estate on the east side of Park, at 4800. This is the Silveira house, built in 1917 by Oakland architect R. A. Hutchison for a local dairy magnate and still one of the area's most elegant private homes. After admiring that, cross to the west side of Park, and start walking downhill on Trestle Glen, past the gates and a sign that warns you are leaving Oakland and entering Piedmont.

Trestle Glen descends rapidly, dividing around a traffic circle containing one tall thin redwood and a couple of magnolias, gradually developing a nice overhang of shade. The homes are statuesque and well-landscaped, and present a variety of styles.

Just after the driveway for a very large shingled home at 1834, find your first staircase on the right-hand side of the street. It begins with seven short steps, between two low stone columns and bordered by a low wall, decorated with occasional saltillo paving stones, and then starts to climb in earnest, rising a sharp 97 steps to land beside 289 St. James Drive. Cross the street, and turn left, noting as you go that the saltillo tile pattern on the steps is repeated on the sidewalks.

Just before you get to the remarkable Japanese-themed house and garden at 288, you see a wide staircase, decorated with those same tiles, rising on the right. This has the look of an abandoned public staircase, or one that has been commandeered by a homeowner. Some stairwalkers have been told the path is private and off-limits to the public. In any case, it rises only a short distance, runs into a redwood tree, and terminates in a driveway. This driveway returns to St. James, so don't waste your time. Instead, walk on a bit, getting a full view of the Japanese garden before coming to a wide traffic island full of big trees. Veer to the right of this, and just after the house at 254, find the crescent-shaped entrance to the next staircase.

This one is, again, elegant, tiled, and beautifully maintained, and rises an impressive 118 steep steps to deposit you at 191 Sandringham Road. Turn left and head downhill, into a canyon rich with mature trees. At the bend in the road, stay left and continue on Sandringham, then turn left where you meet Cambrian Avenue. Pick up good views of downtown Oakland here, as well as the port and the Naval Air Station at Alameda, as you descend Cambrian. Then, just after the house at 77, find another crescent-shaped entrance, and your next staircase.

This one begins as a narrow walkway, leading to 38 steep steps down to St. James again. You'll see the traffic island you passed earlier, and beyond it your previous staircase, over to the left. If you want to squeeze in some extra stairs, return and take another lap. Otherwise, turn right and walk along St. James.

Admire the fine trees and expensive landscaping, past newer and less enormous houses, as St. James winds along. Pass

Croydon Circle on the right, then turn onto St. James Place on the left—ignoring the "Not A Through Street" sign as you go. This cul-de-sac street will drop a short block, and reveal, next to the Norman-influenced house at 60, your final staircase.

It's a big one—a very steep drop of 110 steps, fitted with a handrail and, as before, decorated with saltillo pavers—dropping you back onto Trestle Glen. If you're a glutton, turn around, climb this staircase, and retrace your steps back to the starting point. If you're not, turn left and begin the trudge up Trestle Glen. It's a little boring, but it doesn't last long. Soon you will pass the first staircase, and soon after that you will see the gates announcing your exit from Piedmont and return to Oakland. This is Park Boulevard, and your starting point.

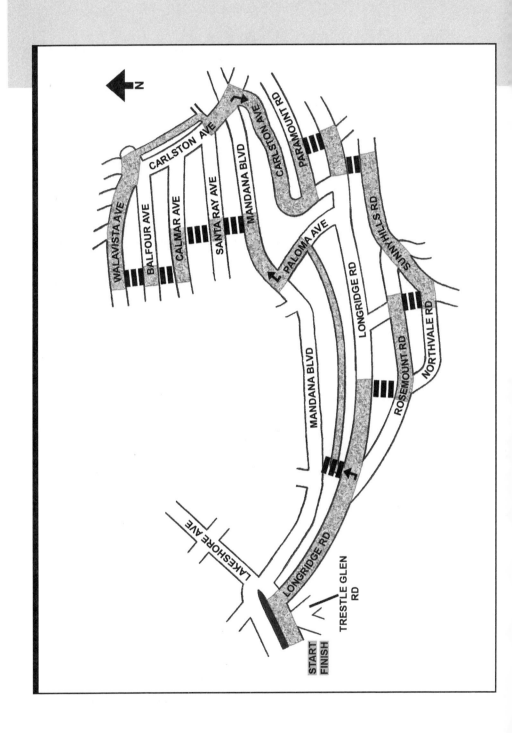

WALK #26

TRESTLE GLEN AND LAKESHORE HIGHLANDS
DURATION: **1 hour, 30 minutes**
DISTANCE: **3.5 miles**
STEPS: **429**
DIFFICULTY: **2.5**
BUS: **606, 26, B**

This is a fairly easy walk through a historic Oakland hills neighborhood filled with stately houses. What it lacks in elevation change it makes up in length and charm, as it includes a couple of unexpected "greenway" trails.

Start your walk in the busy commercial Lakeshore Avenue district, which offers a profusion of pre-walk destinations—among them Peet's, Starbucks, Noah's Bagels, Trader Joe's, an outlet of the worker-owned co-op Arizmendi, and even the 24-hour Colonial Donuts, where the men play chess night and day. Heading north on Lakeshore, cross Trestle Glen Road, then turn right onto Longridge Road, passing through the iron gates that mark the beginning of the historic Lakeside Highlands development.

　　The trestle in question was a railroad bridge built by Oakland's noted Frances "Borax" Smith's trolley company, which extended a line from downtown Oakland into a green area then known as Sather Park—in memory of the same Peder Sather from whom Cal's Sather Gate gets its name. The railway made it possible for another entrepreneur, one Walter Leimert—whose son later developed a section of Central Los Angeles, called Leimert Park, which still bears his name; Walter has a street named after him nearby, over on the other side of Park Boulevard—to develop a new residential area known as Lakeshore Highlands. Ads from 1922, which called the development "the best place for the San Francisco Man to live," promised potential buyers a commute of only nine minutes from downtown Oakland and 36 minutes, by rail and ferry, from San Francisco. Two sons of New York's Central Park designer Frederick Law Olmstead were hired to design the landscape of the development. Those iron gates were designed by the same firm that did San Francisco's City Hall building.

As you walk along you'll note at once an interesting mix of architectural styles, from the exaggerated porch on 606 to the rough stucco statement of 671. The houses become somewhat statelier as you climb. At the "Y" intersection with Rosemount Road, pause in the little triangular park to read up on the local history, or enjoy one of the handy benches. Then return to Longridge (the left side of the "Y"), cross the street and, between the houses at 704 and 708, find the gravel footpath that marks the top of your first staircase.

The Trestle Glen staircases are not marked or named. This one drops into a woody bower, bordered by chain link, down 31 concrete steps, landing at an intersection with a pathway that comes in on the right. Stop here, and turn onto Oak Grove. This is a charming greenway, perhaps half a mile long, that parallels Longridge above and Mandana Boulevard below. It winds in and out of the shade of oaks, redwoods, loquats, figs, spruce, and pine. Wider here, narrower there, its redwood-chip walkway offers a welcome respite from concrete.

In time the greenway ends at Paloma Avenue. Turn left and head sharply downhill, to land on Mandana. Cross the street and turn right, heading uphill. Note as you go the front-yard vegetable gardens at several houses, where tomatoes and peppers are in profusion in late summer. Note too the fine liquidambar trees overhead, turning red and gold in fall.

Just past the white picket fence bordering the house at 800, turn left into the pathway. Take the long sidewalk approach up a gradual rise, eventually climbing six wide steps, to land beside 805 Santa Ray Avenue. Cross the street and jog slightly to the left, to continue up a set of wide concrete stairs for a total of 140 steps, landing at 805 Calmar Avenue, where the peak is marked by a fine spreading date palm.

Turn left and walk along Calmar, past a stretch of quietly modest homes. Just before the most striking of them, a large oxblood-red structure at 786, turn right and climb five stairs into a narrow pathway. After 50 feet, begin the descent down 59 rather uneven concrete steps to land at 4128 Balfour Avenue. Then cross the street and immediately find another staircase, this one dropping an impressive 105 wide concrete steps, without a handrail, to deposit you on Walavista Avenue.

I don't know what a "wala" is, and perhaps you won't see one here. But turn right anyway, and begin a slow ascent. At the top of the block, you will find a complicated intersection where Walavista meets Balfour and Carlston Avenues. Walk straight ahead, keeping Walavista on your left and Carlston on your right, aiming directly for the sign that reads "Notice to Dog Owners." Here you will find the beginning of another greenway path.

Walk straight on, bordered by a redwood fence on the right and a concrete block wall on the left, into a deeply shaded overhang of untended trees. In time the path will meet another at a "T" intersection. Turn right and walk about 100 feet. You'll find yourself back in civilization, at the corner of Carlston and Santa Ray.

Turn left and walk downhill on Carlston. At the bottom of the hill, cross Mandana again. If you're ready for a rest, enjoy the little park to the right. If you're ready to break the rules, look for the pleasantly-named Slug Steps on the left side of Carlston. This is a beautiful staircase that rises to Paramount Road, but it shows signs of water damage and erosion, and for some time has been barricaded against entrance. It is a delightful climb,

WOODEN STAIRS ON AN OAKLAND HILLSIDE.

but not recommended. Instead, walk up Carlston, rising to the corner of Paramount, and make a hard left. As you go, enjoy the increasingly comfy houses, like the Georgian-style 733 and the fine tile work around the door at 649. The houses become even comfier and more self-conscious on Paramount. ("This is Crocker Highlands," a friendly neighbor explained.)

Just after the house at 853, on the right-hand side, find the narrow sidewalk leading to your next staircase. This one is a sloping passage with 10 steps dropping down to Longridge. Turn right, and walk along a flat stretch of road, admiring the almost-twin Tudors with scalloped eaves at 984 and 987. Just past the second of these, on the left hand side of the street and across from a fine, massive redwood, find the next staircase—a drop of 24 steps that culminates between two white picket fences and deposits you at 968 Sunnyhills Road. Turn right.

Here are big trees and big houses. Walk along to the "Y" intersection and bear left, continuing down Sunnyhills. At the next "Y" intersection, veer right onto Northvale. Moments later, just after the house at 872, find another staircase on your right. Climb a series of 22 concrete steps to return to Rosemount. Turn left and walk along Rosemount. Northvale will merge from the left. Cross the street here and, just after the house at 800, find your final staircase. It contains 27 steps and a length of sidewalk, and will deposit you back on Longridge once more. Turn left and walk along a section of flat street, past the little triangular park you visited near the beginning of this walk. In time Longridge will begin to slope downward, gently returning you to Lakeshore, through the Trestle Glen gates, and back to your starting point.

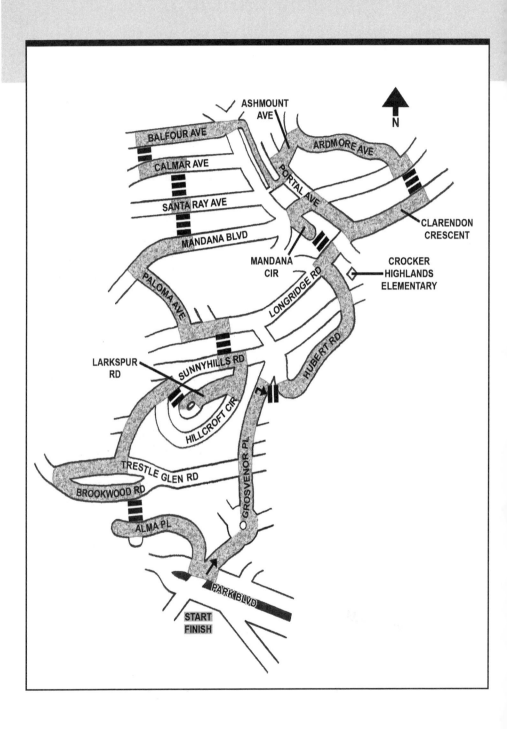

WALK #27

TRESTLE GLEN AND CROCKER HIGHLANDS
DURATION: **1 hour, 30 minutes**
DISTANCE: **2.8 miles**
STEPS: **470**
DIFFICULTY: **4–4.5**
BUS: **18, 618, 688, V**

This is an awesome walk involving fancy neighborhoods and falling-down staircases. Though probably a poor idea on a rainy day, it's an arduous combination of refined and rustic, and a great workout.

Begin this walk on Park Boulevard, just north of the 580 freeway, at the complicated intersection where Park meets Excelsior Avenue, Alma Place, and Grosvenor Place. Find the top of Grosvenor and start walking straight ahead and downhill. You'll pass an Oakland DWP substation on your right and descend into a neighborhood of well-kept homes and leafy streets. Continue downhill past the traffic roundabout, and past the turning for Trestle Glen Road.

Trestle Glen got its name from a long-ago railroad bridge that helped Oakland residents get into the then-undeveloped hinterlands for picnicking and revelry. The trolley line ran from downtown Oakland, up Park Boulevard, to about Grosvenor, when it turned toward Underhills Road. It crossed the hollow into which you are now descending, and carried passengers across the hollow into a green space known as Sather Park—all long gone, the trestle and rail line having been dismantled by 1906.

Cross Underhills Road, noting the handsome half-timbered house at 950 (dating from 1926, a little sign says) and the turreted round structure at 953. Then, just after the house at 976, find a narrow pedestrian passage on your right. This is a sloping asphalt path, well-landscaped and private in appearance, that rises some distance, climbs nine steps, and drops you at the end of a paved driveway. Walk to the end of the drive, and arrive on Hubert Road. Turn right and walk uphill, past increasingly grand homes, fronted by an impressive array of ornamental fruit trees.

Hubert levels out and bends left, past a pair of well-placed sidewalk benches on the right-hand side of the street, and then meets Sunnyhills Road. Cross the street, walk past Crocker Highlands Elementary School, and continue until you meet Longridge Road. Cross the street to the opposite corner, but then turn right at once onto Longridge. Two houses in, just past 1116, find your next staircase.

This one begins as a sloping sidewalk, then under deep shade develops into a 41-stair drop down to the cul-de-sac end of Mandana Circle. Walk downhill, out of the circle, and turn right onto Mandana Boulevard. Walk uphill a short stretch, then turn right onto Clarendon Crescent. This rises a long, arching block past smaller, handsome houses, crossing Longridge and bending left. After a bit the road levels, and then drops down, passing another handsome half-timbered house at 1089. Then, between the houses at 1092 and 1096, find two steps and a handrail on your left, and your next walkway.

This one passes a tree house and a huge redwood tree before falling five wide steps down onto Mandana Boulevard once more. Walk straight across Mandana—pausing to glance at the good downtown Oakland views straight down the boulevard—and enter Ardmore Avenue. This is another long block of well-designed homes. It rises, falls and bends, and the sidewalk on the right-hand side of the street lifts high above the roadway.

Enjoy the elevation and then, where Ardmore meets Ashmount Avenue, turn left and head downhill.

You meet Portal Avenue after a very short block. Turn left, and then look at once for the narrow pathway just after the big brick house at 839. It runs tight between two houses, and halfway along—you can see the next street just ahead of you—meets another narrow pathway. It's a pathway intersection! Turn right onto this new path, and walk about 100 yards through a very pleasant urban forest, heavy with tree and leaf and shade.

You emerge at another complicated intersection, the crossing of Walavista Avenue, Carlston Avenue, Balfour Avenue, and Park Lane. Take a soft left onto Balfour, and walk up a slight slope. The road flattens out and presents a long block of newer, less exotic homes. After the big one at 4128, catch your next flight of stairs. This one's a mess—overgrown, with extremely uneven risers, and no handrail—and for that reason has a fine rustic charm. Climb 54 steps, carefully, to a flat patch of broken-up sidewalk, and then drop five steps down and turn left onto Calmar Avenue.

Cross the street and climb a slight rise. Just before you arrive at the impressive palm tree growing at 815, find the steps going down on the right. Descend a fine wide staircase, bordered by an attractive low wall, falling 130 steps to the sidewalk and another 10 down to the street. This is Santa Ray Avenue. Cross the street and continue your descent, taking the path that slopes down to a final six-step drop back onto Mandana Boulevard. Turn right. Walk down Mandana a stretch, then, before you reach the stop sign, turn left and climb Paloma Avenue. It's a sharp climb. I apologize. It can't be *all* stairs.

Just after the house at 631, on the right, you may note a driveway leading to a small park. This opens into "Oak Grove," an amazing wide green belt—heavily featured in Walk #26, Trestle Glen and Lakeshore Highlands—maintained as a piece of public land. That's for another day. For now, continue up Paloma.

At the crest, cross the street and turn left onto Longridge Road. Admire the many Norman- and Tudor-inspired homes

here. Just after the one at 983, grab the staircase going down on
the right. It falls 23 steps, in deep shade, to land once more on
the same Sunnyhills you passed an hour ago. Turn left, then turn
right immediately onto Hillcroft Circle. Bear right at once onto
Larkspur Road.

This is a charming street of faux-cottages and hacien-
das, but it doesn't last long. Shortly you will come to a wide traffic island filled with trees. To the right side of this, between the
houses at 924 and 911, find the staircase going down—topped by
a handy bench. Drop down 58 steps to land at the intersection of
Hillcroft and Sunnyhills. Take a left and begin walking downhill
on Sunnyhills.

You'll pass a turning for Northvale Road and a strange
garden full of volcanic rock at 877, and then run into Trestle
Glen Road again. Turn right and walk a long flat block until you
reach a stop sign. Turn hard left and climb up Brookwood Road.

This is a one-way street and you're going the wrong way,
so watch the traffic as Brookwood rises and then flattens out. Up
and to your right is the unseen, but very audible, 580 freeway.
As Brookwood begins to descend, watch closely on your right to
find, just after the house at 1079, your final staircase.

This one is another mess, a wooden ruin of broken
stairs, broken handrails and, on wet days, slippery mud. But
what a staircase! A sign at the bottom says "Closed." A sign at the
top says "Closed." But in fact the staircase is open. Proceed with
caution, and at your own risk. Climb 127 steps—more or less; it's
hard to tell when so many steps are broken or missing—to arrive
at Alma Place.

Turn left. Walk a short block of this modest residential street, past pollarded plane trees and a trio of incongruous
palms. Shortly, Alma will curve to the right and bank down to an
intersection—with Grosvenor and Park, and your starting point.

Overleaf: A VIEW OF THE BAY, BRIDGE, AND CITY FROM THE OAKLAND HILLS.

PART FOUR

OAKLAND: THE NORTH AND WEST

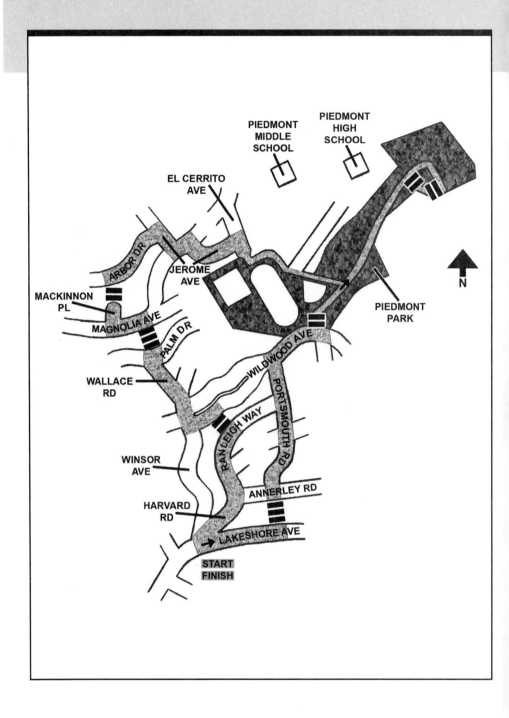

WALK #28

LOWER PIEDMONT PARK
DURATION: **1 hour**
DISTANCE: **1.8 miles**
STEPS: **176**
DIFFICULTY: **3**
BUS: **26**

Piedmont Park is one of the East Bay's loveliest spots, a heavily wooded glen filled with secret delights. This walk winds through the lower part of the park, collecting staircases and interesting architecture along the way. To extend it, pair this stroll with Walk #29.

Start this walk near the triangular intersection of Lakeshore Avenue, Winsor Avenue, and Harvard Road. Bear to the far right and walk up Lakeshore, past the stately deodara cedar on one side of the street and the magnolia on the other. Pass a number of modest homes, many of them stucco variations on Craftsman lines, and just after the house at 4079 find your first walkway on the left.

This is the signposted Portsmouth Walk, which rises seven steps up to a sloping walkway that lifts you to the corner of Portsmouth and Annerly Road. Walk straight ahead onto Portsmouth, following this pleasant street as it winds down and around, crossing Harvard and then Ranleigh Way. Here you will see a steep slope rising before you, and a sign that says, "Not A Through Street." Ignore both of these discouraging elements and climb up.

At the top, closed to autos but open to you, turn right

onto Wildwood Avenue. Walk along, admiring the delightful cottage and grounds at 308, and the Spanish *finca* at 314. At the next corner, where Wildwood meets Prospect Road, cross Wildwood into Piedmont Park. A marker on your left gives a little history lesson: On what is now the football field far below you once stood a fine old English-style living maze, built in 1908 and meant to mimic the one enjoyed by our royal cousins at Hampton Court.

After you've admired that, walk down the 48 big concrete steps heading straight down. Turn right onto the pathway, heading into the shade of the park, watching for a baseball field to appear on your left. Follow this path as it enters Piedmont Park proper, into the deep shade of redwood and oak. Filled with pathways, an "off leash" dog run, and a panoply of spots for strolling, contemplation, or canoodling, this 15-acre park is a beautiful expression of civic pride. Stay always to the left as the path winds and rises. In time you will come to another historical plaque. This one marks the location of Sulphur Springs, a park attraction with healing properties dating from the 1860s that once attracted the likes of Mark Twain.

Walk on, past this, following the path as it rises and hugs close to the creek below. Then, where the railing ends and the trail hairpins back on itself, make a hard right turn and climb up the side of the hill. Follow this pathway until it merges with another path coming in on the left. Shortly after, a short staircase appears on your right. Drop down 13 stairs, cross the creek, and then turn right down yet another short staircase, this one dropping nine steps down onto a sloping path that leads to a T-intersection. Turn left, and retrace your steps back toward the baseball field.

Where the road makes a "V," bear right, with the baseball field on your left. Follow the road along as it rises, passes an entrance to the football stadium, and heads into the school grounds—both Piedmont Middle School and High School share this hillside above you—and winds around to the left. Stay on the roadway, and stay on the left. The road will descend again, and the football field will come into view. Continue down until you come to a stop sign. Turn right, and head up a slight slope, out of the school grounds and onto El Cerrito Avenue.

Walk up El Cerrito a short distance, then turn left onto Jerome Avenue. Walk along Jerome until it bends right and meets Magnolia Avenue. Cross Magnolia carefully at the corner, turn left, and walk a short block. Then turn right onto Jerome again. Walk downhill the length of one very short block, and turn left onto Arbor Drive. Descend this long, quiet block, shaded by good liquidambar trees, but keep a close eye out. Just before you reach the traffic roundabout ahead, and just after the house at 116, find your next passageway on the left.

This is a narrow walkway, rising up to the left, shaded enough that the stairs are mossy even in warm weather. They rise 48 steps to land you at the cul-de-sac end of MacKinnon Place. Walk a short block to meet Magnolia again. Cross the street, and turn left. Climb a little rise, admiring the ancient, handsome Hudson if it's still parked in the driveway there, and then find your next staircase after the house at 144.

This narrow passage drops 10 steps down onto a sloping sidewalk, shaded by oaks, which delivers you to the intersection of Palm Drive and Wallace Road. Walk across Palm, and climb Wallace up a sharp bit of hill. At the top, you will find yourself at the complex crossing of Wallace, Winsor, Wildwood, and Warfield. (Why do developers and urban planners *do* this?) To the degree this is possible, walk straight ahead across the intersection, and then turn left onto the *downhill* side of the split-level Wildwood.

Walk a very short distance, past only the first house, and then find the next staircase on your right. This one drops a quick eight steps onto a slope, and then drops another 33 steps to deposit you again on Ranleigh. Turn right, and walk along as Ranleigh turns and bends to the right, becoming Harvard Road. Follow Harvard along. After a short distance you will find yourself back at the large triangular lots that separate Harvard, Lakeshore and Winsor—and back at your starting point.

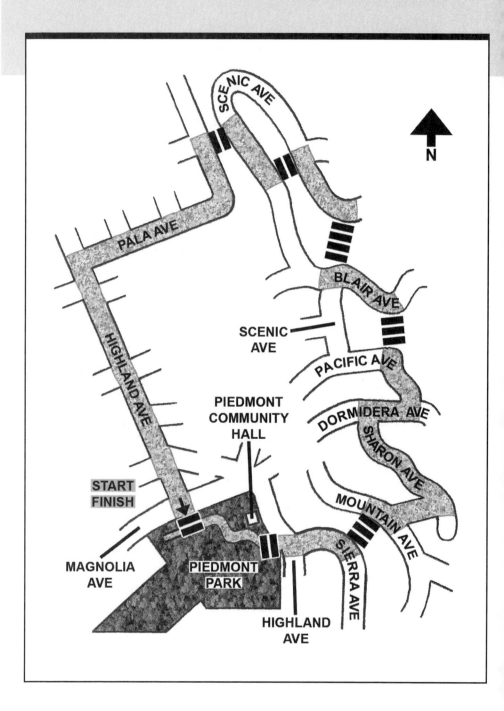

WALK #29

UPPER PIEDMONT PARK
DURATION: **1 hour**
DISTANCE: **1.6 miles**
STEPS: **482**
DIFFICULTY: **3.5–4**
BUS: **11, P**

Like its Lower Piedmont sister, Walk #28, this walk includes a stroll through one of California's prettiest city parks, and also includes marvelous homes and probably the best bay views in the Oakland hills.

Begin this walk near the top of Piedmont Park, at the intersection of Highland and Magnolia Avenues. You'll find a police station and civic center here, as well as the massive gates, framing a large urn, that mark the entrance to the park. Leave the car or the bus and start there.

A helpful plaque here explains that the sloping ground before you was once the site of the Piedmont Springs Hotel, which served guests of the Sulphur Springs attraction deep in the canyon below. The hotel was built in 1872 by a man named Walter Blair, and was very hot stuff for 20 years, until it got too hot and was destroyed in a fire.

Enter the park and start walking down the wide stairs—16 steps down to a fountain, then six more, then a batch of 55 more, until the stairs end in a "T" intersection. Take a left, walking along a narrow sloping pathway, until you cross the creek. On the other side, turn left, and head uphill, and take six steps up.

Bear left. You'll hear tennis balls bouncing high, up to the right and meet a municipal building (Piedmont Community Hall) just ahead. Walk to the right of this. Past it, hidden in lovely shrubbery, is a Japanese tea house, with a fine rock garden behind it. Keep this close to your left, following the

narrow pathway, until you meet a set of stairs. Climb 11 steps up to the street.

Here you find the intersection of Highland and Sierra Avenue. Walk straight ahead, across Highland and onto Sierra, taking note of the huge sycamore trees above you and the fine houses around you—Piedmont was once known as "The City of Millionaires," because it boasted more of them per-square-foot than any city in the United States—like the Monticello-style at 11, for example, and the huge bungalows at 17 and 20.

Then, just after the house at 17, turn left and climb four steps into a shady pathway. This will carry you between two large houses and deposit you across the street from a massive home fitted with wide porches at 255 Mountain Avenue. Turn right, but just barely, and then turn left right away onto Sharon Avenue.

Sharon climbs sharply, past a substantial brick home at 64, and then begins to bend to the left. (The no-exit Sharon Court goes off to the right here.) Climb up some more, until Sharon crests and begins to fall. You could sneak a peek at the bay, between the houses,

A secret staircase beneath the Oakland trees.

from here. But don't. Better views are coming. At the next corner, where Sharon meets Dormidera Avenue, turn right. Climb
some more, then turn left onto Pacific Avenue. Take note here
of a very stately brick and shingle Craftsman at 221, which has
either been beautifully preserved or beautifully restored.

Pacific rises, flattens, and begins to fall sharply down
and to the left. *You*, however, continue to rise, onto the big staircase straight ahead. Catch the walkway turning in at the bend
in the road, and climb a concrete staircase, fitted with a handrail running up its spine, that rises 68 steps to land on Blair
Avenue—named, perhaps, after the founder of the Piedmont
Springs Hotel.

Turn left, and downhill, and begin now to really appreciate the major bay views. From here is a vista from Lake Merritt
on the left to Sausalito on the right—with an overlapping of the
Bay Bridge and the Golden Gate Bridge dead ahead. On winter
afternoons you can watch the sun go down directly behind the
Sutro Tower high atop San Francisco's Twin Peaks.

For now, though, begin to descend on Blair, losing the altitude you just gained. But shortly after, as Scenic Avenue comes
in on the left, look for a staircase on the right. The good news is
that you get your altitude back, and the big views that come with
it. The bad news is that you have to climb to do that—149 steps
straight up, along a concrete staircase split by a steel handrail.
You'll note a Phoenix Iron Works manhole cover at the bottom of
the staircase, and again halfway up, and again at the top. Think
about this, and breathe deeply as you climb.

At the top, turn left onto the aptly named Scenic Avenue
and walk along a flat section of roadway, enjoying again some
very wide views of the bay below. At the charming traffic circle
dead ahead, with a giant evergreen supporting not less than four
children's swings, and just after the house at 308, find the next
staircase. This one goes *down*, giving you back the altitude you
gained a few minutes before, dropping a mighty 112 steps, fitted
with double handrails. Note as you go the roof-top observation
decks on some of the homes, and take a cue from them: Stop and

enjoy the view as you descend.

You land on another stretch of Scenic. Turn right and walk along a short piece, passing the former home of writer Jack London at 206—perhaps not the original London home, but the site of it—and a big castle at 224. Then, just after the house at 227, find the staircase on your left. (Don't worry, it's *down* again.) Descend 48 steps and a sloping sidewalk to land at the elevated sidewalk above Pala Avenue, at the corner of Pala and Park Way. Drop down seven more steps to street level, and turn left onto Pala.

This is another sycamore-lined street of stately homes. Follow it as it bends to the right and drops down three blocks—past a fine Craftsman at the corner of Monte Avenue—until you meet Highland. Turn left and walk along this busy boulevard, perhaps slowing to admire the fine corner house at 1900 Oakland. Further on there are handsome school buildings on the right, as well as handsome bank buildings. At the next corner you'll find a church, a gas station and, across the street, a Veterans Memorial Building with an honor roll of local soldiers who died in World War I, World War II, Korea, and Vietnam. Housed in the same building is the Piedmont Police Department. And, just after that, straight ahead, is the park itself—and your starting point.

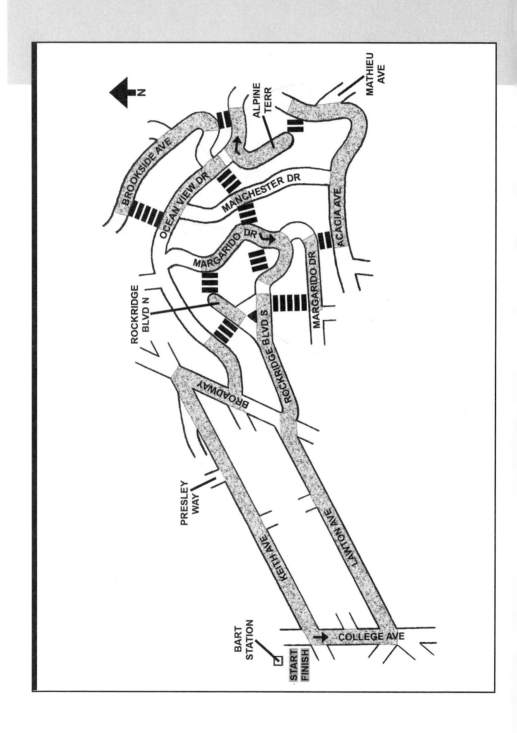

WALK #30

UPPER ROCKRIDGE WEST
DURATION: **1 hour, 30 minutes**
DISTANCE: **3.2 miles**
STEPS: **593**
DIFFICULTY: **4**
BUS: **51A, 51B, Rockridge BART**

This is a fairly rigorous walk from the Rockridge flats to the Rockridge heights, through streets that survived the devastating 1991 fires to streets that have risen from its ashes. Stunning architecture and stunning views.

Begin your walk along Rockridge's College Avenue with a high-end delicacy from Market Hall, a snack from Cactus Taqueria, or a coffee or beer at one of the neighborhood's many cozy spots. Then walk south on College—with the BART station behind you—and turn left onto Lawton Avenue.

The bustle of College ends and two long blocks of small, elegant homes begin. Note particularly the almost-matching Craftsman beauties at 5537 and 5533, and the clinker-brick touches at 5566 and 5581. A concrete stamp in the driveway at 5587 reads "V.B. DECARLO, 4.10.1923," which gives you an idea of the age of this neighborhood.

When you reach busy Broadway, use the crosswalk to get to the eastern side of the boulevard. To your right is stately brick St. Peters Church. To your left are the stately concrete and stone gates to Upper Rockridge.

Turn left, walking between the imposing gates, onto Rockridge Boulevard. Note the line of very tall, very old palm trees ahead of you, and the fine-looking old houses on both sides of the street. Bear right, as the street meets a large triangular park, onto Rockridge Boulevard South. Then, just past the house at 6095, find the almost-hidden staircase that is your first climb. It is long and wide, but not so steep, rising 75 steps without a handrail to land on Margarido Drive. Note the antique-looking light fixture at the top of the stairs. A stamp at its base indicates it's the work of United Iron Works, and probably original to the area.

Take a left, and begin walking uphill on Margarido, noting the old houses around you. Then look high up to your left to see the new McMansions on the hillside there—a stark difference between the part of Rockridge that survived the terrible 1991 fires and the ones that have been built since. It was a brutal burn, costing 25 lives and more than 3,500 homes. The fire started due north, along the ridge where Tunnel Road and Highways 13 and 24 converge. Blown by hot, dry "Diablo" winds, it blazed downhill and over the Rockridge crest, leaving ashes in its wake. On some streets, only the sidewalks and staircases survived.

As you walk along, note the big pink house at 5900 with the good-looking tiles framing its front door. Then, just after the house at 5918, find tiny Quail Lane on your right. It's just as quaint as its name suggests (though I saw no quails) and rises as a wide staircase, split by a handrail, up 42 steps and a steep sloping sidewalk.

You land on Acacia Avenue. Turn left, noting as you go the concrete stamp in front of the house at 6000. It reads, "V. Dizillo," and dates from 1935—decades before the house itself, a fire replacement, was built. Stay on Acacia as it crosses Manchester Drive and winds around to the right, admiring the remarkable little forest of Japanese maple on the hillside to your left. Pass Verona Path—not for today, but included as part of Walk #31—and press on. Cross Mathieu Avenue, coming in on the right. Then, ahead on the left, find Locarno Path.

This is an elegant and very elderly staircase, wide and sweeping, with uneven and broken risers, so historic in feeling that it might have been imported directly from its Swiss namesake. You could be a glutton and dash down lower Locarno to Cross Road, and back up. Or you could be sensible—leaving those for a later attempt on Walk #31, too—and take upper Locarno, climbing 62 steps to land at the cul-de-sac end of Alpine Terrace. This is Rockridge's highest point. Walk ahead to the vacant lots on the left, if they're still there, and enjoy some massive views—from downtown Oakland and the port on the left-hand side, to Pt. Richmond on the right-hand side, and the Golden Gate and Bay Bridges rising somewhere in between.

Walk down Alpine as it descends and passes the curiously-named "The Istana," the nicely-tended corner house on the left. ("Istana" means "palace" in the Malay language, and is the official name for the President's residence in Singapore. Here, it must be someone else's palace.)

Turn right onto Ocean View Drive. When you reach the vast rose-colored lighthouse house at 6183, with its maritime weather vane, cross the street and find the top of Brookside Lane. This is a charming walkway, dropping through a series of landings—the middle one fitted with stone benches—and 62 steps beneath some lovely redwood trees. The rails are new in construction; the stairs are clearly older. Turn right, where you land, onto Brookside Avenue. Wander downhill, as the roadway curves and bends. Pass a stately old lone redwood tree at 6376, and skip the right turn onto Eustice Avenue, continuing down Brookside.

Below on the right is probably the brook that gave the street its name. Also below are the redwood bungalows that make up the campus of College Preparatory School. The bungalows once housed students of the Oakland public school system, but were bought in the 1970s—at a price of $130 each!—and moved to CPS's six-acre campus off Broadway.

Above, on the right, note a line of old homes and old trees rising high above the hillside. Of particular interest are the eucalypti that seem to be suspending in air the house at 6273. Then, just after the mailbox at 6251, find the bottom of Claremont Path. This one rises 65 steps and a steep stretch of sidewalk to deposit you on Ocean View Drive once more, at the corner of Manchester. Turn left and walk uphill. Dig the energetic use of iron work in the front yard at 6138—did someone get a welding torch for Christmas?—and climb up as Ocean View gradually earns its name.

Ahead you can probably see the street sign for Alpine Terrace. Before you get there, though, look to the right, just after the subtle, shingle-roofed house at 6143, to find the bottom of the staircase known as West Lane. (It has a sign, somewhat hidden by the liquidambar tree growing next to it.)

Climb 16 steps and a rose-colored sidewalk—the work, a concrete stamp indicates, of Schnoor and Son—up and over the Rockridge ridge. Behind are the East Bay hills; ahead are the flatlands and the bay. Drop down a final 25 steps, with a rather unsteady handrail, to land on Manchester Drive. Cross the street and continue onto another flight of steps, called Prospect Steps. These are wide and rose-colored again, and drop, without benefit of handrails, 76 steps into Margarido-ville once more.

The steps continue ahead, but you don't. Drop down three stairs to the sidewalk level, then turn left before starting a long descent. Walk along Margarido as the road divides and the right half begins to drop. Follow the roadway down and around. Just after the house at 6150, you'll find the bottom of Prospect Steps. Look sharp—it's a little hidden—and turn into the driveway between 6150 and 6140. Walk up, admiring the Provençal themes on the house to your left—and the nice tiles over the window—to approach the bottom of the stairway. Then climb a sharp 48 steps, under a giant palm tree, to land on Margarido again.

Did we walk down just to walk up? Yes, we did. This is a stair book! That's why we're here!

Turn left and walk along the Margarido sidewalk as it bends and swings around. Then, just after the boxy red-tiled house at 6033, find the top of the Margarido Steps. This is a re-cently-restored staircase, with bright shiny handrails and many new sections of stairs, dropping 72 steps (not counting the eight separating street from sidewalk, at the top) onto the cul-de-sac circle of Rockridge Boulevard North.

Walk through the circle, keeping to the right-hand side. Note ahead and below you the line of very old palm trees and the triangular Rockridge Park that you passed at the beginning of this walk. Just before you get to that, though, and just after the house at 6100, find another Schnoor walkway (rose was evi-dently their specialty) off to your right.

Climb 47 steps up a wide staircase split by a handrail, under deep palm tree shade, past a bench halfway up, to land on Ocean View for—I promise—the last time. Walk left and down-hill until you meet Broadway, and exit the Upper Rockridge de-velopment. Turn right onto Broadway, and walk uphill a block to the intersection with Keith Avenue. Cross the busy boulevard with the traffic light, and walk along Keith as it fronts the off-ramp from howling Highway 24.

Keith used to be a lovely street, before the motorway came and spoiled things. On your left are some fine old homes, increasing in beauty as you pass Presley Way and approach Rockridge's commercial district. There is a pair of nice red-wood homes at 5909 and 5907, and a very stately Victorian-era mansion, fronted by a sturdy stone wall, at 5825. (Check out the pipes servicing the upstairs bathroom, evidence that this beau-tiful pre-1900 house was built without indoor plumbing, and probably had an outhouse out back.)

Cross McMillan Street and admire the long line of stucco Craftsman homes as you near your destination. Check out, too, the fine home at 5681 and the handsome trio of redwood trees at 5669. On your right you will see the parking lot for the BART station. Just ahead is College Avenue. Turn left, and find your starting point.

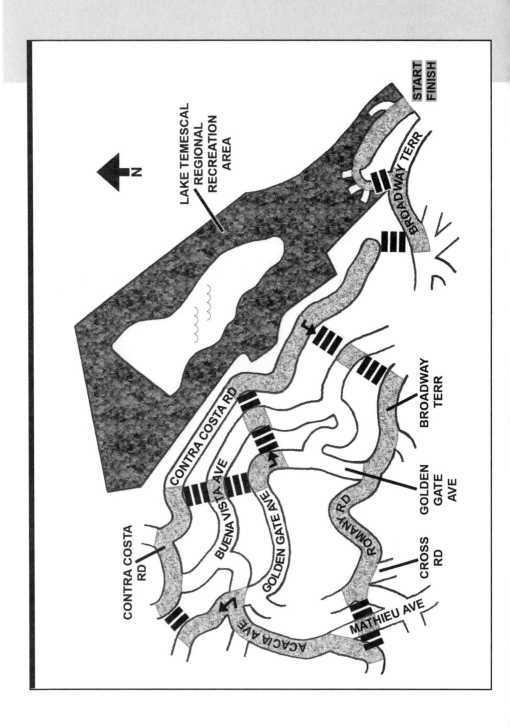

WALK #31

UPPER ROCKRIDGE EAST
DURATION: **1 hour, 15 minutes**
DISTANCE: **2.4 miles**
STEPS: **742**
DIFFICULTY: **4**
BUS: **682, 688, 605**

This big walk begins in a lovely lakeside park and traverses the ridges of Upper Rockridge, surveying the historic homes that survived the 1991 fires and the newer ones replacing the homes that didn't. Along the way are surprising views of Oakland and the bay.

Begin walking from the Lake Temescal Regional Recreation Area. (Parking is free except on weekends and holidays, when a $5 fee is collected at the toll booth.) If you have time, tour the park, check out the lake and do some fishing. (Actually, if you have that much time, you probably aren't reading this book.) From the bottom of the parking lot, with the restrooms and park buildings over to your right, start up the wide dirt path to your left. Follow it to the first turning, about 50 yards in, then take the switchback-dogleg to the left. Climb up beneath dense redwood shade until you meet a redwood handrail. Then climb four redwood risers and step cautiously onto Broadway Terrace. Turn right and walk up the sidewalk running uphill. The lake you've left behind was the creation of one Anthony Chabot, who in 1868 dammed up Temescal Creek and created a reservoir that held drinking water for the city of Oakland—an act that helped encourage population growth in the city.

Busy Broadway Terrace rises, crests, and begins to fall. As it does, watch on the right, just after the house at 6370, for Erba Path. This is your first staircase. Climb 80 steps, interrupted by stretches of sloping sidewalk fitted with a handrail, to land at the cul-de-sac end of Contra Costa Road.

A plaque set in the sidewalk praises the life and work of Ruth Parkinson Williams, a local resident who was evidently a big part of the resuscitation of the community after the 1991 fires, which started in the hills to the north and blazed down, and into Rockridge. You may note that the staircase you've just come up is quite old, but the houses around you are quite new. The staircases, sidewalks, and some of the light standards are among the only structures that weren't burned down on some of Upper Rockridge's streets.

Turn left and walk along Contra Costa. Take advantage of the vacant lot, if it's still there, to dig the huge views of Oakland and the bay. As you go, note on the right an impressive Tudor-influenced home at 6232, with an enormous brick chimney, flanked by tall eucalyptus trees. This is one of the few upper Rockridge houses spared by the flames. Note also the staircase driveway, a rarity in this region. Almost next door, at 6200, is a replacement version of an Edwin Louis Snyder home. The original was said to be a great example of Snyder's Spanish Colonial Revival design. The current dwelling was rebuilt along these lines after the fire.

Just after the house at 6201, find the next staircase on your left. This is Arbon Path, a wide stairway split by a steel handrail and anchored in the middle by a great old oak tree. It is beautifully landscaped and well-maintained, and drops over many levels for a total of 132 steps.

You land on Buena Vista Avenue. Cross the street, admiring the big views and the one lone palm standing sentry in the vacant lot on the right, and continue down Arbon Path. Drop down 66 steps, over multiple landings, without benefit of handrails, to land on another section of Broadway Terrace. Across the street is Ostrander Park, a long, slender sliver of green running downhill.

Turn right, along Broadway, and walk along the park. You'll note the homes here are older and statelier, and are pre-1991 construction—survivors. At the "Y" intersection just ahead, bear right and uphill onto Golden Gate Avenue. Then turn left at the first corner, using the crosswalk leading into Romany Road. Stay to the right-hand side. There on the curb, on the corner, you will see a curiosity: An old stamp in the concrete dates the sidewalk to 1918, and indicates that the *original* names of these two streets were McAdam and Hays. According to some very helpful folks at the Oakland Public Library's Oakland History Room, Hays Avenue became part of Golden Gate Avenue in 1911, and McAdam became Romany Road in 1898. That's how old this neighborhood is.

Wind downhill on Romany beneath some older oak trees, staying on the elevated sidewalk on the right-hand side of the road. The homes are older now, too, as Romany levels out and bends to the left—note the tiny home vineyard and lavender farm at 6016—and then descends to an intersection with Cross Road. Cross Cross, going straight ahead, and then look at once to the right-hand side of the road. You'll find the bottom of your next staircase.

This is Verona Path, another stately old stairway, rising up 52 steps and a sloping sidewalk, split by a handrail, to land on Mathieu Avenue. Cross the street, jog slightly to the right, and continue up, climbing another 21 steps and another sloping sidewalk, to land on Acacia Avenue. Turn right and walk along this street of newer homes. You may start to notice now the old green-tinted light standards, each with a pendular octagonal lantern. Occasionally you will see a newer, black light standard, sometimes with the same lantern planted on top of it. Occasionally, it's the same black lamppost, with a newer globe stuck on it. Along this stretch, walk as you cross Mathieu and, after a bit, come to the elegant entrances to Locarno Path.

But, don't go there. Save that for another day, and

another walk—Walk #30, Upper Rockridge West.

For now, continue straight ahead. Cross Ocean View Drive and then, as Acacia bends right, turn left onto Golden Gate. Note again an old cement stamp in the sidewalk—marked "1913 The Oakland Paving Co."—reminding you that Golden Gate used to be called Hays Avenue. You pass newer and much bigger homes now, many of them with fine northwestern views of the bay. Just after the big one at 5499, cross to the right-hand side of the street and catch the next staircase—up the 31 short steps that make up Gondo Path.

You're on Buena Vista Avenue now, and the other side of Rockridge. The west-facing bay views have turned to east-facing hill views. Above and ahead of you are the steep slopes topped by Grizzly Peak and Skyline Boulevards. Lower down, and unfortunately quite audible, is Highway 13, aka Warren Freeway. Turn right and climb Buena Vista as it bends uphill. Here are big new homes with big old ideas—like the proto-Victorian with the wide porch at 5860 and the faux-adobe Mexican right next door.

Bear left where Buena Vista meets Contra Costa Road, ignoring the "No Outlet" sign. Climb Contra Costa and turn to appreciate the fine views. Almost all of Oakland, city and port, are visible here, as is the top end of historic Mountain View Cemetery, final resting place for many of Oakland's famous residents.

Bear right past the turning for Contra Costa Place, as Contra Costa Road flattens and bends. Then, just after the house at 5991, catch a staircase going *down*. This is Chaumont Path, which falls steeply, but without handrails, 77 steps from top to bottom, giving off better views of Mountain View Cemetery as it goes. You land on Buena Vista again. Cross the street, as Chaumont Path continues—dropping another 48 steps past a nice-looking shingled home on the right, with abundant fruit trees and a fig arbor in its backyard.

Turn left onto Golden Gate Avenue, and you can already see your next staircase. It's a half-block ahead, on the left, and bears the curious name of Belalp Path. (It's probably named after the Swiss ski resort, a high mountain, auto-free village that can be reached only by cable car.) This one is long and wide, fitted with a handrail, and rises 76 steps under heavy oaky shade. The top, covered by liquidambar trees, is a little uneven and a little untidy, and has a nice rustic feel to it.

Cross Buena Vista again and continue on to upper Belalp, wishing by now, perhaps, that *you* had a cable car. Climb a series of uneven stairs, with a crooked handrail, up 71 steps and a steeply sloping sidewalk, to land on Contra Costa once more. Turn right. Appreciate the flat roadway now as Contra Costa winds along, past a huge turreted tower at 6116, catching big cemetery and city views down to the right. Shortly, you will pass Arbon Path, also on the right. Ignore this—you've done it already—and continue along until Contra Costa nears its cul-de-sac terminus. There, almost invisible after the house at 6351, find the top of Erba Path.

Drop down 80 steps. Land on Broadway Terrace again. Turn left, and walk uphill, over the crest and down the back side. Watch for the redwood handrail on your left, then take the four steps and steep trail back down into Lake Temescal Regional Park. Make the dogleg right onto the main path, and return to the parking lot and your starting point.

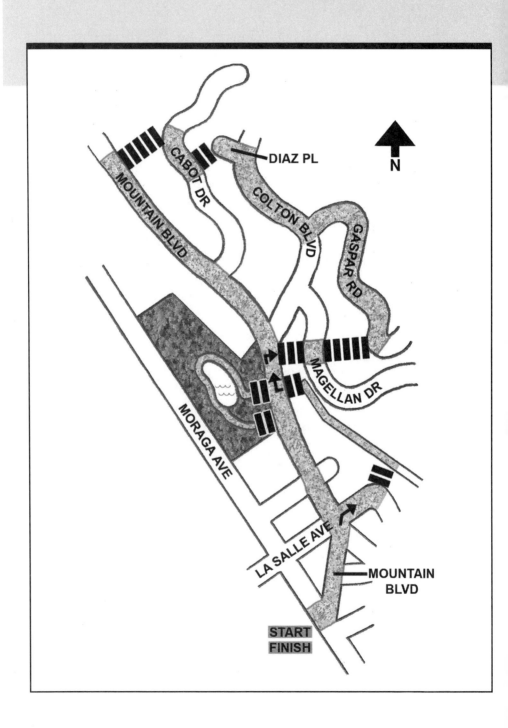

WALK #32

MONTCLAIR VILLAGE
DURATION: **1 hour**
DISTANCE: **2 miles**
STEPS: **693**
DIFFICULTY: **3**
BUS: **18, 61, 688, 605, CB, V**

This is a short but strenuous walk up and down the south-facing hills of Montclair. It features a charming village, a quaint city park and, on Sundays, a large farmers' market.

Begin your walk in Montclair's little commercial district, near the intersection of Mountain Boulevard and Moraga Avenue. Walk up Mountain, into the village, where you will find a pair of pit stops: Starbucks on your left, and Peet's on your right.

When you are fortified, turn left turn left past the Starbucks, walking west on Mountain, then turn right onto La Salle Avenue and climb a slight grade. At the top of this, where La Salle ends beneath a white flagpole, head left to find your first staircase. Climb six stairs to a steep paved ramp, and head up the right side of the ramp to the woody walkway.

This is an old railroad right of way. (On some maps it's identified, in fact, as "Montclair Railroad Trail.") Trains used to run along here, part of a line that connected Oakland to Sacramento. At one time it was going to be used for a freeway, until environmentalists and locals protested. Now it is a bike path and hiking trail, running several miles east, to the right, up into Shepherd Canyon.

For now, though, go west, walking with the Montclair business district on your left. Cross a pedestrian underpass, left over from the train days, that gives residents from the hillside access to the business district. Continue straight ahead as the bike path (marked on posted signs as bikeway #8) turns down and left. Walk on, into a fine glade of tall eucalyptus, staying on the left side as the path nears a commercial building. Aim for a staircase with green handrails on the left. Drop down 15 steps to land on Mountain once more. Turn right and walk to the first corner, where Colton Boulevard comes in. There, on your right, find your next staircase.

It's a big one, a towering concrete-with-handrails set of 143 stairs that zig-zags over multiple landings to lift you up to Magellan Drive. You land opposite a big shingled house at 1840. Cross the street, and just to the right of this house you will find the continuation of your climb. So, climb!

This is another big one, also a zig-zaggy concrete-with-rails structure. It rises a mighty 188 steps, between growths of agave, Spanish broom, and oak, finishing along a redwood fence, marked with graffiti, and under a big plywood tree house. You might catch a glimpse of the Cal Campanile between the branches if you turn around and look over to the right.

At the top, you arrive breathless at 1957 Gaspar Drive, the cul-de-sac end of a steep slope that continues up the hill. When you've got your wind back, begin up this slope, but turn immediately left onto Gaspar. Stop there and, if it's clear, enjoy the good views of Mount Tamalpais.

Wander downhill a bit, past cliffhanging modern houses and hillsides rich with oak and eucalyptus, until Gaspar meets Colton. Cross Colton carefully—traffic moves fast on this street—turn right, and walk uphill slightly. At the bend in the road, find Diaz Place on the left. Turn in and take this to its cul-de-sac end. It appears to go nowhere, but, between the houses at 15 and 21 you'll find...stairs!

This set goes down, for a change, but is another sturdy concrete-with-handrails design on a zig-zag pattern. It drops 98 steps down through good shade—accompanied by the increasing noise of the nearby 13 Freeway—to deliver you to 5680 Cabot Drive. Turn right and walk along Cabot, past a selection of interesting homes.

Where Cabot bends to the right, you bend to the left. Sandwiched tightly between the houses at 5707 and 5711, find the hidden staircase. Like its Montclair brothers and sisters, it's a concrete construction with handrails, on the same zig-zag pattern, but it also features brick and concrete benches at each landing. Drop down 179 steps to land beside the imposing structure at 1650 Mountain—the Montclair Woman's Club—and across the street from the charming structure at 1687—the storybook, slate-roofed Montclair branch of the public library. Turn right, walk to the corner, and cross the street with the light. Then turn left, head uphill, and begin the return journey along Mountain.

In time you will pass the elementary school, some tennis courts, and a handball court. On your left, where Colton comes in, you'll recognize your first big staircase. Walk on, past some tennis courts and a high cement wall. Where the wall ends, turn right into the city park. Take 38 stone steps down, past another tennis court, to the lakeside pathway.

The water fowl collection here is impressive. You may view it by circumnavigating the lake, going right and around its back side. Cross the waterfall, or climb above it, if it's flowing. Walk past a sandbox and some play structures for the kids, circle the back of the lake, and return toward town, passing some picnic tables. Then head for the baseball diamond. Behind the backstop and the bleachers, under some heavy redwoods, find another set of stone stairs. Climb up a final 26 steps to return to Mountain, and turn right. If it's a Sunday, between 9:00 a.m. and 1:00 p.m., turn onto La Salle and visit the farmers' market. If it's not, walk straight ahead, and follow Mountain back to Moraga, and your starting point.

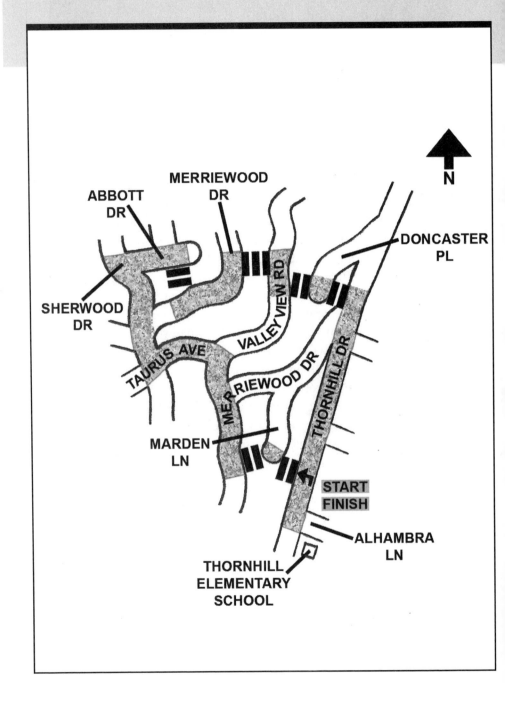

WALK #33

MERRIEWOOD
DURATION: **1 hour**
DISTANCE: **1.2 miles**
STEPS: **637**
DIFFICULTY: **4.5**
BUS: **61, 602, 642, 688, CB, V**

This is an all-wood stairwalk, a delightful hike along the sides of heavily wooded Merriewood, up and down a collection of massive wooden staircases. Like a walk back in time, it is probably the most rural walk in this collection, and one of the most strenuous, and one of the most beautiful.

Begin your walk on Thornhill Drive, near the corner of Alhambra Lane, in front of Thornhill Elementary. Cross to the west side of the street and walk up Thornhill, keeping the school on your right. Just after the house at 5915, find your first wooden staircase, the Merriewood Steps, on the left.

These stairs, as well as most others in the area, are marked by a sign reading "Public Staircase." This is helpful, since many of the houses here can only be reached by staircase, and many of the private staircases are built of the same redwood as the public ones. Walk toward the sign and begin climbing—up a sharp 72 risers, past redwood fences and wild berry vines, to land at the cul-de-sac ending of Marden Lane. Across the cul-de-sac, painted in fire-engine red, you'll see the continuation of these stairs. Grab them, and climb on—up another 117 steps to land at 5612 Merriewood Drive.

Catch your breath. Turn right. Walk along Merriewood, enjoying the trees (this area was spared in the terrible fires of 1991) and the eccentric houses, many of which are old and appear to have been built with hand tools. Overhead are mossy oaks and abundant bird life, and below are fine canyon views.

This should keep you occupied until you reach the first intersection. Veer left onto Valley View Road. After a short stretch, make a hard left turn onto Taurus Avenue, which takes an even sharper rise to a wide, flat intersection. Then turn right onto another stretch of Merriewood. Walk uphill slightly and, after about 75 feet, bear left onto Sherwood Drive. Follow this road uphill, past the imposing brick-bottom castle on the right, at 5916 Sherwood, pausing to admire its turrets, leaded glass and eccentric ornamentations, and to take in, behind you, some fine views of Oakland and the bay. Then follow the castle's property line around to the right and onto Abbott Drive.

Take this short, steep street only a short bit. Where the road splits, just after the house at 35 Abbott, find the marked staircase going downhill on the right side. This is a slight variation on the preceding wooden staircases. It starts with a series of wide platforms, separated by redwood railroad ties, dropping you 40 broad steps down to a wooden staircase, fitted with handrails, that falls an additional 18 steps.

You are now on Merriewood once more. Turn left, and walk slightly uphill. Just after the house at 5960, find another marked public staircase on your right.

This one is very steep indeed, another all-wood affair, fitted with rails, that falls an extremely sharp 123 steps to land at 6086 Valley View. Turn right and head downhill the width of one lot, and then find another super-steep staircase on the left. This is another sharp drop of 75 stairs, softening to a railroad tie walkway and another series of stairs, falling another 93 steps to deposit you onto the cul-de-sac end of Doncaster Place. Cross the pavement, and find one final staircase.

It's one more big steep one, all-wooden and fitted with double handrails, running between redwood fences over a series of 99 steps to land at the corner of Thornhill and Merriewood. Turn right, onto Thornhill, then cross the street carefully and head downhill along the creek, past a series of flower and vegetable gardens, until you reach Thornhill Elementary, and your starting point.

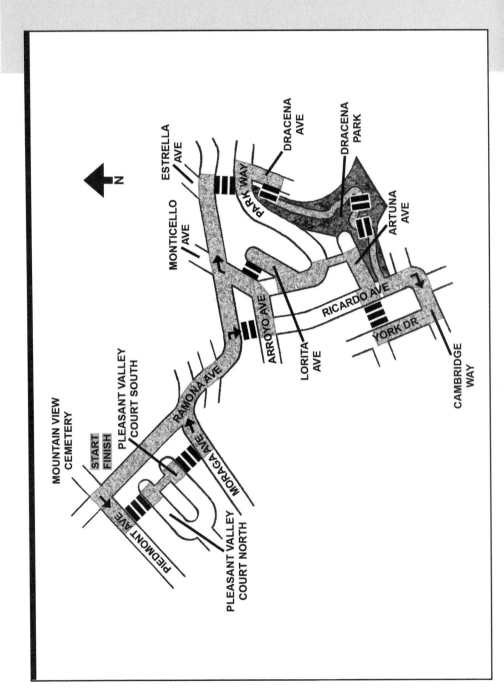

WALK #34

DRACENA PARK
DURATION: **1 hour**
DISTANCE: **2.1 miles**
STEPS: **152**
DIFFICULTY: **2**
BUS: **12, C**

This is one of the oddest, most unexpected and most beautiful short walks in this collection—the unexpected beauty is in the unexpected combination of a cemetery building and a city park. This walk would also connect nicely with Upper Piedmont Park, Walk #29, for a longer outing.

Begin your walk at the northernmost reaches of Piedmont Avenue, in front of the Chapel of the Chimes mausoleum at the doors of Mountain View Cemetery. Take time, if you have it, to explore this remarkable, if strange, Julia Morgan-inspired edifice. Inside are columbarium rooms containing the ashes of the deceased, some of them resting eternally in bronze "books" lining the walls of a "library." There are interior gardens, rococo ceilings, stained glass ceilings, ceilings open to the elements, live songbirds singing, and more. Marvelous.

When you are sufficiently impressed, cross the street and walk down Piedmont, with the cemetery gates behind you and the chapel on your right. Just after the building at 4476, find a narrow walkway to your left. Take this between the buildings, down 12 wooden steps to a concrete walkway, until it meets

Pleasant Valley Court North. Cross the street, continue onto another walkway, and meet Pleasant Valley Court South. Cross the street again, and enter a final walkway. This one will culminate in 17 wide concrete steps, split by a steel handrail, up to Moraga Avenue.

Turn left and walk uphill, past the turning on the left for Ramona Avenue, as Moraga bends right. Just before the huge stone sign on your left for Mountain View Cemetery, cross Moraga in the crosswalk, and continue straight ahead down Ramona. The road slopes down gently, crossing Ronada Avenue beside a beautiful old Craftsman with a freestone foundation and chimney. As Ramona curves to the left, cross the street and find a short staircase on the right. Climb up 15 stairs, with a rail, and follow a short path. This will deposit you at 65 Arroyo Avenue.

Turn left and walk to the corner. Where Arroyo meets Monticello Avenue, turn left again, and where Monticello meets Ramona, turn right. Walk up this quiet stretch of fine-looking old homes. Just after Estrella Avenue comes in on the left, and just after the house at 300, find your next staircase on the right.

This is a series of 10 steps down, onto a path running beside a fine lush fern garden that leads to 11 more steps down to Park Avenue. Turn left onto Park, then turn right at once onto Dracena Avenue. Then find a staircase on the right, dropping down into Dracena Park—nine steps down into the redwood-filled gully.

Take the path downhill to the left, then choose the middle path, avoiding the smaller paths on either side, and find yourself in an amazingly dense redwood forest—a mini-Muir Woods of fine tall trees—as the trail drops down and down. The path will end in time at a low gate. Walk through this, and bend left into the second section of the park. Follow the sidewalk as you pass some stone columns, with a playground over to your right.

Ahead is as lovely a piece of city park as any in California. On some maps, it's known as Dracena Quarry Park, which would explain the depth of the park and its steep walls. The quarry was

owned by Walter Blair, who built the Piedmont Springs Hotel
and a nearby dairy. He quarried stone from this site to build
homes in the area.

Follow the path around to the left as it circles a fine
grassy glade, shaded by huge old oaks, redwoods, deodara ce-
dars, pine, and Japanese maple. When the path has wound all
the way around this Edenic bowl, find the concrete staircase,
fitted with handrails, leading up to the left. Climb 17 steps almost to street level and then—because this *is* a stairs book—find
another staircase going back down on the right. Fall a final 39
steps back to the lower park level. Turn left onto the pathway
and wander down to the end of the park, where you meet Ricardo Avenue. Turn left onto Ricardo. Cross El Cerrito. Walk to
the next corner, and turn right onto Cambridge Way. Then turn
right again at the first turning onto York Drive. Midway down
the block, just after the house at 102, and exactly where Holly
Place comes in on your left, look to the right and find a sidewalk
running between the houses.

Walk up this sidewalk and take 14 steps up, continuing between redwood fences onto a length of asphalt driveway.
When you meet the sidewalk, you are on Ricardo once more.
Cross Ricardo and walk straight ahead, along Artuna Avenue,
keeping to the left side of the park. Between the houses at 33 and
37, rising to your left, find the next pathway. This is a sloping
sidewalk, without stairs, that lifts you from Artuna to another
stretch of Monticello. Turn left, past a series of very good looking bungalows, and then at the first corner turn right onto Lo-
rita Avenue—making sure it's the first corner, because the street
sign is not visible.

Here, as you rise, the houses become grander. On the
near left-side corner is a massive, shingle-sided Craftsman
with a rounded face. Further up the block, take special note of
the charming matched set of clinker-brick and shingle two-
story residences at 24 and 28. Then, when it looks as if the street
is about to end, just after the shingle-sided garage at 21 on the
left, you will find a very narrow, private-looking sidewalk path.

It curves around *behind* the garage, turns left and then right, and hugs close to the back of the house to drop down eight steps and land you once again on Monticello.

Turn right and head uphill half a block, then turn left onto Ramona once more. The road descends, bends to the right, and begins to rise, passing again the fine freestone Craftsman at the corner of Ramona and Ronada. Cross Ronada again and meet Moraga. Cross this busy boulevard carefully at the crosswalk, turn left, and then turn right into the quiet extension of Ramona. Walk straight on a long block, past the modest houses, until you meet Piedmont once again. The cemetery gates are to the right. The Chapel of the Chimes is straight ahead. You are back at your starting point.

Overleaf: A north bay view from Albany Hill Park.

PART FIVE

EAST BAY
& BEYOND

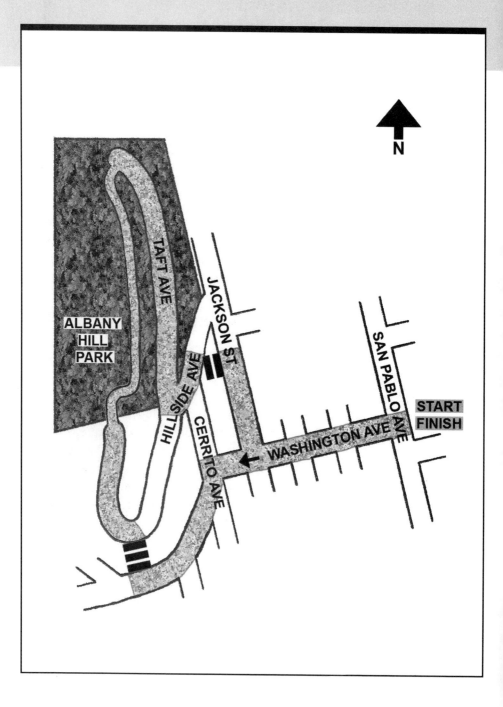

WALK #35

ALBANY HILL
DURATION: **45 minutes**
DISTANCE: **1.5 miles**
STEPS: **155**
DIFFICULTY: **2.5**
BUS: **18, 72, 72M, 800**

Here is an entirely unexpected walk, with fantastic bay views and a stroll through a tiny chunk of forest—in a most unlikely neighborhood. Perfect for a sunset stroll, it offers more trails than staircases, and it's also freeway-close.

Begin your walk to the northwest of Berkeley in the community of Albany, along the main drag of San Pablo Avenue, near the intersection with Washington Avenue. Start with breakfast at famous Sam's Log Cabin, or perhaps a highball from the evocative-looking Club Mallard or Kingman's Ivy Room. Then walk up Washington, going west, heading for the hill. Cross many presidential-themed streets—Adams, Madison, Jackson, and Cerrito, one of the lesser-known presidents—bearing slightly left, then take the right-hand fork in the road to continue on Washington and pass Polk.

Behind you are the Berkeley hills. Ahead of you and left is downtown Oakland. But don't waste your time on these views; much better ones are just ahead. Instead, continue up Washington as it winds around to the right and suddenly at its crest reveals…an amazing western vista.

Here the bay and the city are spread out before you with surprising immediacy. Directly below is the bustle of the 80/580 freeway, running alongside the railroad tracks that carry Amtrak trains to and from Sacramento. Just beyond is the huge oval of the racetrack at Golden Gate Fields. And, just on the right, marked by a charmingly faded wooden sign, there are steps known locally as Catherine's Walk. This masterpiece of a staircase starts in concrete then becomes a stately redwood structure, climbing over multiple flights a total of 100 steps to land on Hillside Avenue.

A vacant lot at the top of the stairs offers even better views to the east and south. All of Berkeley and Oakland are before you. When you've soaked that up, walk uphill on Hillside. After 100 feet or so, another vacant lot offers you another set of stunning views. In addition to the aforementioned pleasures, now you also get the Albany Bulb, Cesar Chavez Park, and, far in the distance, the Golden Gate Bridge. A friendly neighbor observed that, during the winter, a crafty photographer can capture the image of the late afternoon sun setting exactly between the central towers of the Golden Gate Bridge—the best shots occurring between Thanksgiving and New Year's.

Continue walking on Hillside as it flattens and descends to a dead end at the base of Albany Hill Park. Walk into a dense forest of ancient eucalyptus trees and find the trail heading to the right and uphill. Follow the trail into a low saddle, framed by very tall eucalyptus trees. On your right are some shingle-sided buildings. Bear left, and follow the trail up the ridgeline.

This is a wide track between tall trees, coming in time to a rather martial-looking cross, erected by the Lion's Club. There are also benches here facing east. You can sit and watch the BART trains running, or find your favorite part of the Berkeley hills. If you're lucky enough to live there, you can say, "Hey, I can see my house from here…."

Continue uphill as the trail becomes steeper. Then, as it begins to flatten, find a long rope swing and some more benches.

Through the trees, as you wander up the path, are fine views of the bay, Angel Island, Mount Tamalpais, the Richmond-San Rafael Bridge, and even San Quentin.

The trail continues wide and flat across a grassy clearing, then begins to descend. Follow it down until it hits a barricade and the cul-de-sac end of Taft Avenue. Take Taft as it bends back toward Albany and gradually gives up the altitude you gained on the eucalyptus trail.

Between the trees now are good views of Berkeley, Kensington, and El Cerrito. The big patch of grass halfway up the hill is Sunset View Cemetery, at the corner of Fairmont and Colusa Avenue. The big patch of green at the top of the ridgeline is Tilden Park, which you might already have met on Walk #12 or Walk #17.

Taft gradually sprouts houses. You'll pass a set of hillside-clinging, shingle-sided structures on the left. Then, where Taft flattens out, you'll meet Hillside Avenue once again. Make a hard left, and head downhill. Just past the turning for Cerrito, on your right, and across from the townhouses at 925–927, find your final staircase, Castro Steps.

This is a concrete one, fitted with double handrails, dropping a steep 55 steps to land on Jackson. Turn right. Follow Jackson along as it passes the Albany Children's Center on the right, and a number of small but appealing bungalows on the left. When Jackson meets Washington, turn left. Walk the several blocks back to San Pablo, and your starting point.

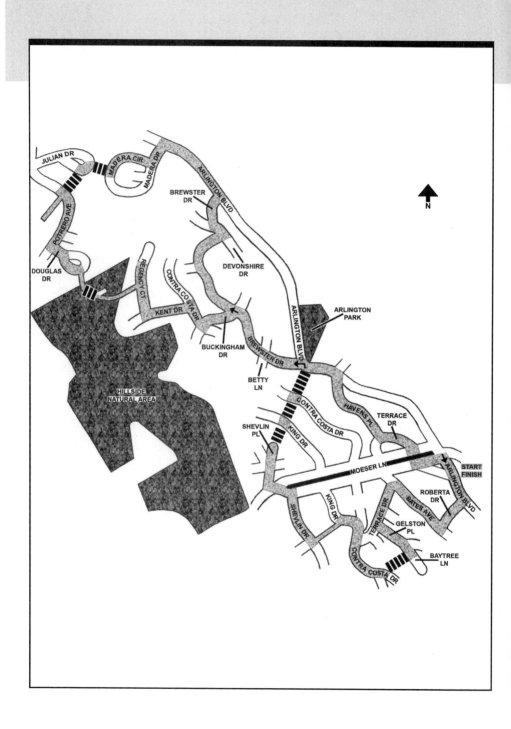

WALK #36

EL CERRITO
DURATION: **2 hours**
DISTANCE: **4.4 miles**
STEPS: **221**
DIFFICULTY: **4.5**
BUS: **7**

This is a long, rigorous walk through the northern community of El Cerrito. It offers hidden pathways, hillside parkland, a blend of old and new architecture, a mix of long, flat streets and dizzyingly steep stairs, and towering views of the top of the bay. If you have time, cap off your walk with a picnic at nearby Blake Garden, an open-to-the-public property owned by the University of California. Access is west of Arlington on Rincon Road.

Begin this walk high above the historic community of El Cerrito, straight north along Arlington Boulevard from Kensington, near the intersection of Arlington and Moeser Lane. Start walking south on Arlington, with the mountains on your left and the bay on your right. Turn right at the first corner, onto Roberta Drive, and head downhill.

Here, descending past a grove of tall eucalyptus on the left, you get your first big views. Don't dally—better ones are coming. Instead, observe the turreted structure just ahead of you. Once known as "Las Mimosas," this Spanish castle was built in 1932 by Dr. Edward Gill, and improved subsequently by Dr. Victor Stallone. It is said to be scheduled for the wrecking ball.

Turn right at Bates Avenue and, as you pass the castle's driveway, turn and salute the armed guard statues standing sentry over it. Walk along Bates the length of a block, and then turn left and downhill onto Terrace Drive, just before you meet Mo-eser. Watch for deer here—I saw the first of several on this walk in the front yard of a house on the right, having Sunday brunch.

Terrace descends, throwing off more big views—the Bay Bridge, the city of San Francisco, and the Golden Gate Bridge in the distance, Oakland far down to the left, and Albany and Albany Hill Park in the foreground. High up to the right is mighty Mount Tamalpais.

The homes are mid-century, but the views are timeless. Walk a short distance and turn left onto Gelston Place, ignoring the "Not A Through Street" sign—that's for cars, not for you. After another short, flat block, bear right and walk downhill onto Baytree Lane.

Keep a sharp lookout on the right. Just after the house at 769, catch the driveway to the house at 763. It looks private, but isn't, and descends past a line of plants potted in old wine casks. Stay left as the driveway narrows to a sidewalk and drops down five steps, with a handrail, onto a sloping walkway. You may note a profusion of cackling chicks and hens on the left, and more big views dead ahead. Walk on, and fall 18 final steps to land at the corner where Highgate Road meets Contra Costa Drive—marked on some maps as another stretch of Terrace Drive. Whatever you call it, turn right, walk past the stop sign, and climb uphill a little. (Watch for wildlife; I saw my second deer here.) Use the crosswalk to get to the north side of the street, turn left, and downhill, onto King Drive.

Note the audio accompaniment of many wind chimes at 915, as King drops and bends around. Look sharp. Between the houses at 929 and 933, find a thin trail descending on your left. This starts between a chain link fence on the left and a redwood fence on the right, with big views of the bay dead ahead. Walk down carefully—in wet weather, the trail might be a little slippery. Bear right where the trail forks, falling now between chain link on both sides, and land at last on Shevlin Drive, where it meets Stockton Avenue. Turn right onto Shevlin and walk along another uneventful stretch of roadway, toward a tall stand of eucalyptus and redwood. The views through the woods are terrific. Just past the tall trees you will see Richmond Harbor, Brooks Island, and Mount Tamalpais presiding over all.

Shevlin meets Moeser. Cross this busy intersection very carefully—the traffic on Moeser will be going fast—then turn downhill for about 30 yards, and turn right as Shevlin Drive continues north. Pass Earl Court on your left and Burns Court on your right, and go straight ahead as Shevlin Place rises before you. Just ahead is the next staircase. Climb up to it, to the cul-de-sac end of Shevlin Place. Then take 11 stairs up to a curvy sidewalk and up 29 more stairs, fitted with a handrail, to land on King Drive. Cross the street and, under a low-hanging oak tree, continue up.

A shady creek appears on the left as three steps rise to a sloping walkway—sometimes a little slippery, if it's wet—to finish with 23 steps and a railing to land on Contra Costa once again. Take a deep breath. Turn and admire the view. Then, continue! These steps aren't done with you yet.

Cross Contra Costa, jog slightly left, and find the trail rising up into deep redwood shade, under low-growing branches, into a green bower of private walkway. Climb five stairs onto a sloping length of sidewalk, past lovely gardens on both sides, up a final 25 wooden steps to land on busy Arlington Boulevard. Breathe deep. Turn left. Walk a short distance. Arlington Park appears on the right. Brewster Place appears on the left. Turn onto Brewster and walk along this flat length of roadway. Appreciate as you go the huge home and property up the hill on your right, where an ancient palm-lined driveway leads to a sturdy Spanish-themed residence. This is the George Friend Estate, designed in 1930 for a prominent local developer by Edwin Louis Snyder, himself another early Cal architecture student of John Galen Howard and contemporary of Bernard Maybeck, et al. Snyder is known as the father of the Spanish Colonial Revival style in the Berkeley area, and this is a fine example of his work.

Walk on. Cross Betty Lane and Buckingham Drive as Brewster continues quietly along, then begins to rise and bend up to the right—bringing on increasingly fine views. At the intersection with Devonshire Drive, turn left and downhill, then pick up Brewster as it continues to the right. After another short block, find busy Arlington again and turn left.

Across the street is a section of the Mira Vista Golf and Country Club, offering an attractive expanse of greens and fairways. Luckily there are many signs posted reading "No Trespassing," making it abundantly clear that you are not welcome to stroll here. So stay on the left side of the street, and walk down the sidewalk to the first corner. Turn left onto Madera Drive, paying no more mind to the "No Outlet" sign than you did the "No Trespassing" signs.

Madera descends a short bit, then offers you Madera Circle to the right. Take this, and descend some more. As the street bends to the left along a line of oak and pine, watch for the house at 1520, and the walkway just after it. Turn right and take the sidewalk to a long run of stairs, down a steep hillside fitted with handrails, dropping a big 98 steps down to land at the circular end of Julian Drive.

Swing around the circle to the left. On the other side, find some more stairs—steep, nosebleed stairs—dropping through a forest of big pines and past a creek bed, down a steep 119 steps. You emerge into magnificent views, onto the roadway at 7704 Portrero Avenue.

I know you're tired, but cross the street anyway. Walk straight ahead, past a warning about "Pedestrians Only," onto a wide green belt passing between the houses and climbing a short distance to a bluff. Once you arrive, you will see it's worth it. The views are simply staggering. Take five. Chill. Catch your breath. You'll need it for the walk back.

Return to Portrero Avenue and turn right, walking downhill. You'll pass a gated driveway on the left, and then come to another left, onto Douglas Drive. Turn here, then bear right as Douglas splits in two. Beside the house at 1520, just after a big sign informing you that deer might be playing nearby, turn to the right onto a wide dirt path running between the houses.

You'll come upon a sign letting you know you are entering a pedestrian walking zone, known officially as Hillside Natural Area. Walk straight on, along a ridge trail, then drop down
four wooden steps to a "T" intersection with a wider trail. Turn
left onto this trail and go uphill, and then keep going uphill.
At times the way is quite steep and the trail zigzags a bit. When
you run into an intersection of trails, stay on the wider trail and
keep going straight up—always heading due east and uphill.

In time you will emerge onto a stretch of flat trail, which
widens and deposits you onto a paved road. This is Regency
Court. To your left you may see a low wooden sign indicating you
are in El Cerrito parkland. (If you don't, but to your left see the
cul-de-sac end of Regency, don't worry. You're on the right road,
but you have emerged from the parkland a little further north.)
Turn right and walk uphill along a block of mostly new, mostly
Mediterranean stucco homes. (Note the curious overhead light-
ing, an interesting mix of old and new.)

The road will rise slightly and meet Kent Drive. Turn left
and walk uphill. It's a climb, but behind you are views to refresh
your spirit. Walk to the first corner, then turn right onto Contra
Costa Avenue. Follow the uphill grade to the first corner, then
turn left onto Buckingham Drive. Climb a little more—just a
little!—and after a block turn right onto Brewster Avenue.

Now the road is flat, and will remain so for the duration.
Continue along Brewster as it crosses Betty. After a bit, you'll
pass again the great Friend hacienda, now on your left. Where
Brewster ends at Arlington, bear right. You'll see the steps you
climbed from Shevlin on your right. Walk past these, up the hill
to the next turning. Go right, onto Havens Place. This will slope
down and around, in time meeting Terrace Drive again, in front
of a handsome barn-like house on your right. Turn left, up Terrace. Walk a curving block. You'll meet Moeser again. Cross it,
carefully, and turn uphill to hit Arlington—where you will find
yourself back at the starting point, and at the conclusion of the
final walk in this collection.

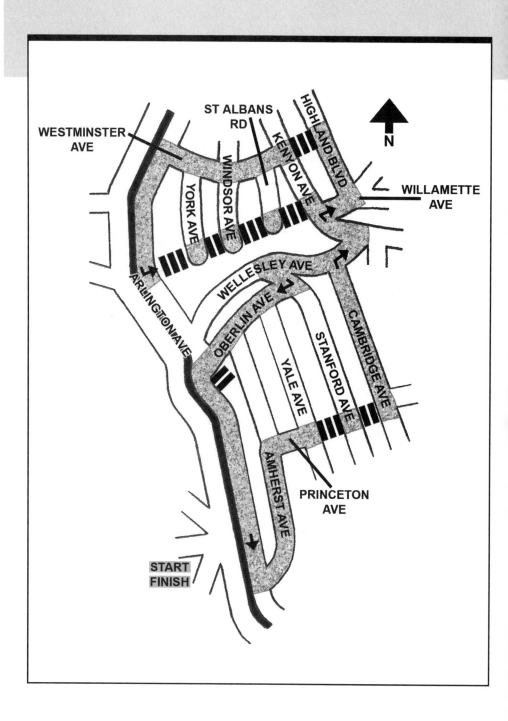

WALK #37

KENSINGTON NORTH
DURATION: **1 hour**
DISTANCE: **1.8 miles**
STEPS: **267**
DIFFICULTY: **3.5–4**
BUS: **7**

This is a symmetrical walk up and down the west-facing slopes of North Kensington. It lacks something in architectural and arboreal delights, but is a good strenuous walk featuring fantastic views. Part stair walk, part trail hike, it's probably not the best choice on a rainy day.

Begin your walk in Kensington's charming little commercial district, with a coffee at The Arlington or a snack from Young's Market. Walk south on Arlington Avenue, toward the ancient Rexall drugstore on the corner, then turn left and walk uphill on Amherst Avenue—the first of this walk's college-monikered streets—into a district sometimes called University Heights. Wander up to the first corner, and turn right onto Princeton Avenue. Walk uphill one short block to meet Yale Avenue. Then, straight ahead, between the houses at 245 and 247, find your first staircase.

Climb 31 steps past a magnificent metal-work gate on the left, continuing up 15 more steps and a steep hillside. It's slippery in wet weather, and could use even more of the steps that the Kensington Improvement Club has been adding to this path. You land on Stanford Avenue. Cross the street and note that the stairs continue—in concrete, now—on the other side. Climb 23 steps and stop for the view, the first of many magnificent vistas, this one with a good look at Point Richmond and Brooks Island. Continue up another 46 steps, fitted at the top with a handrail, to land on Cambridge Avenue.

Take a left onto Cambridge, enjoying the views as you descend slightly. There is Mount Tamalpais; there, Point Richmond; and there, to the left of them, is the large hummock of land marking Albany Hill Park, featured in this volume as the centerpiece of Walk #35. Cambridge descends gradually and meets Wellesley Avenue. Turn right, and walk uphill a short block. Then turn left onto Kenyon Avenue, past the massive outcropping of rock at the corner house.

(Note also the concrete stamp from Schnoor Bros. This company poured a huge amount of the concrete sidewalks in the East Bay area, and its stamp can be seen on dozens of area streets.)

Kenyon is a quiet, flat stretch of road. It curves to the right and then meets Willamette Avenue. Turn right, and after a short block turn left, onto Highland Boulevard—a grand name for a simple hillside street. Walk along Highland, admiring the curvy drive and sloping lawn at 163, keeping a sharp eye out for the next turning.

It comes just after the house at 160, and at the time of this writing was a narrow, overgrown trail leading down to the left. A drainage project was underway when I first walked here, and the trail was wet, uneven, and slippery. If it looks dodgy, skip it, and instead walk straight ahead on Highland until the next corner, then make a sharp left-hand turn onto Kenyon. Walk along Kenyon until you meet Westminster Avenue, and turn right.

But if the trail is passable, watch your footing and continue downhill. The path passes narrowly between the houses, under a heavy overhang of shrub and tree, to drop 11 steps into the front drive of the house at 59 Kenyon.

Wipe your shoes and walk straight ahead onto Westminster Avenue, heading straight downhill. You'll cross St. Albans

Road, Windsor Avenue, and York Avenue before meeting Arlington Avenue once more. Take a left, walking downhill on a stretch of rose-colored sidewalk. Just before Arlington meets Sunset Drive on the right, just past a big white adobe with a low wall dotted with Mexican tiles on the left, find a massive set of steps just past the house at 163.

At the base of the steps is another curiosity—a concrete stamp in the sidewalk, undated, reading "Arlington" and "York." (Kensington locals say the original staircase was built in 1912 by J.H. Spring Company.) Above you is a long, shady staircase, recently restored by the Kensington Improvement Club. It rises 84 steps to the cul-de-sac end of York Avenue. On the opposite side, under low-hanging branches, find the next staircase. It starts as 29 redwood railroad tie risers and becomes a redwood-chip walkway, passing between two faded redwood fences and ending next to a house on the right with redwood siding. You land on the cul-de-sac end of Windsor Avenue. Cross the circle, again, and enter a grassy path, heading up the slope, passing narrowly between the houses at 133 and 135. (Hats off to the folks who keep the grass so nice and trim. Thanks!) At the top are 24 steps, delivering you to the cul-de-sac terminus of St. Albans.

Cross the circle, yet again, and find the narrow path between the houses at 125 and 141. Walk close to the handsome English Tudor on the right, up a path through deep ivy, and across some scattered paving stones to land on Kenyon once more. Take a right. Shortly you'll pass Willamette—yes, you *have* been here before. When you meet Wellesley and that dramatic rock outcropping, turn right and walk downhill, staying on the right-hand side sidewalk, which will rise high above the roadway, increasing the fine views of the bay.

The sidewalk ends. Cross Wellesley to the left, onto Stanford. Walk a block of Stanford and turn right onto Oberlin Avenue—your final campus destination. At the bottom of the hill, turn left onto Arlington, walking up four steps to stay on the sidewalk. After a few minutes, you'll be back at the commercial strip and your starting point.

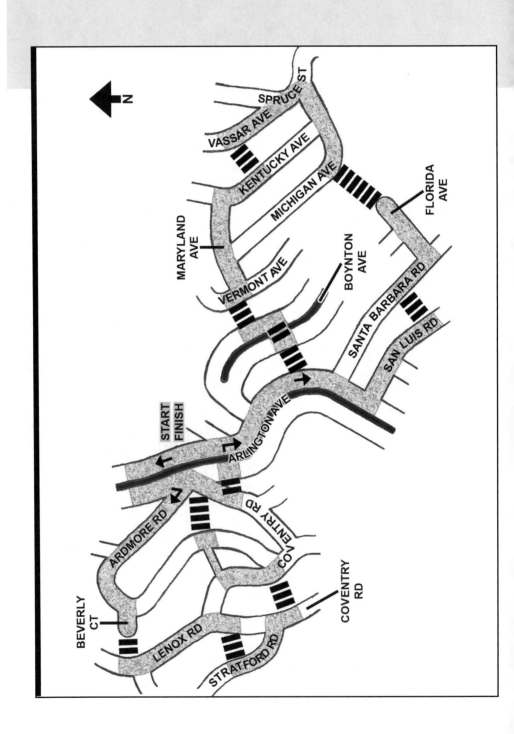

WALK #38

KENSINGTON FIGURE EIGHT
DURATION: **1 hour, 30 minutes**
DISTANCE: **2.7 miles**
STEPS: **340**
DIFFICULTY: **4**
BUS: **7**

This is a looping, overlapping walk that circumnavigates the quiet hillside community of Kensington. It's steep in sections, but the hiking pays dividends in staggering bay views.

Initiate your walk in the little commercial district of Kensington, along divided Arlington Avenue, perhaps with a piece of fruit from old-timey Young's Market, or coffee and a snack at The Arlington. Then walk north on Arlington, past all the shops and offices, to the crosswalk. Walk to the lower half of Arlington, then turn left, and reverse direction to begin walking south. At the three-way intersection ahead, hang a hard right and head downhill on Ardmore Road.

Like many communities in the East Bay hills, Kensington was served by an electric street car—part of the Key System, which ran along Arlington Avenue from Berkeley until the late 1940s. The streets along it were laid out on terraces, with staircases connecting some of them. Some of those stairs are dead ahead.

This is a neighborhood of modest, well-kept homes.

Stroll downhill, bearing left where Ardmore meets Kingston. Cross Kingston, and after the house at 87 Ardmore, watch for the marked Beverly Court on your right. This passage starts as a paved cul-de-sac lined with houses, then becomes a narrow walkway that slopes down and drops eight steps onto Lenox Road. Take a left under the fine spreading oak, and follow Lenox up to the "T" intersection with Coventry Road. Bear right and, just after the first house, with the yellow brick wall, find the unmarked opening of Stratford Path on your right side. Turn into it, and head downhill, crossing four steps and a sloping sidewalk, then nine more steps. You'll pass a backyard ornamented with a gazebo and an ancient fig tree, then land on Stratford Road. Turn left and walk along until Stratford "Ts" into Coventry again.

Turn right onto Coventry and cross the street. Just after the house at 640, find Coventry Path going uphill. This starts rather badly with a bumpy step or two, then offers 17 steps (partly assisted by a handrail) and a long sloping uphill sidewalk, and then another set of seven steps to bring you to the other side of the looping Coventry. Cross the street and turn left. After a short distance, and just past the house at 719, turn right into Ardmore Path.

This is another sloping sidewalk, heading uphill and crossing Ardmore Road before continuing its climb. Under shading oaks, the path meets a fine double-wide staircase, split by a heavy handrail, which leads you 29 steps up to the lower section of Arlington Drive. Bear right, crossing Coventry one last time, and climb the 18 redwood railroad tie steps up to level ground. You're back on Arlington.

Across the street is a handsome old Rexall Drugs sign. Cross here, turn right, and walk past the hardware store and downhill on Arlington. Walk past the turning for Boynton Avenue, using the steps to stay on the sidewalk. Ignore for the moment the staircase known as Boynton Walk, which comes just after, and continue past Santa Barbara Road and turn left onto San Luis Road.

Enjoy this modest neighborhood of solid homes and big

trees. Then, between the houses at 597 and 601, find Santa Barbara Path on your left. This begins as seven steps up from the sidewalk, then continues up a gradual incline along a concrete walkway between yards and fences. Climb up another 10 steps, over the crest, and follow the path to Santa Barbara Road, where it emerges between the houses at 572 and 576.

Turn right onto Santa Barbara. Walk along another pleasant stretch of road to the corner, then turn left onto Florida Avenue. (Across the intersection, if you're a stair fanatic, you may climb the six additional steps up to the elevated sidewalk in front of the corner house.) Walk uphill, past the left-hand turning for Boynton Avenue, past the sign saying "Not A Through Street." Florida ends in a cul-de-sac.

When you get there, find Florida Walk, just to the right of the barn-red garages on the left-hand side. This is a very steep set of 32 steps, with a good handrail and some welcome shade, leading to a hundred yards of steeply sloping sidewalk, dropping you off on Michigan Avenue. (You would know that even if you couldn't find a street sign, because of the helpful contractor's stamp in the top step before you.)

Turn right onto Michigan and continue uphill, calmed by the knowledge that this steep section of street is your final climb. Cross the street and walk past Kentucky Avenue and approach Spruce Street—perhaps using the nine handy sidewalk steps as you go. Behind you is the view that reminds you why you climbed this high. Magnificent!

At the top of the hill, where you've met Spruce, you can look to the right and see a path down into Dorothy M. Bolte park. This is the starting point for Walk #17, and offers a welcome bench, grassy picnic area, and working drinking fountain.

Otherwise, turn left onto Spruce. Walk but a short distance and bear left onto Vassar Avenue, staying on the uphill side of the divided road. Where the division ends, just after the house at 460, find little Holmes Path on your left. This is a gentle, sloping sidewalk that culminates in 12 steps and drops you on Kentucky Avenue—another terraced, divided roadway.

Jog slightly left and cross Kentucky, taking 10 wooden steps to the downhill side. Turn right, walk a block, then turn left onto Maryland.

Here are more fine views of the bay, Mount Tamalpais, Point Richmond, and more. On a clear day, you see almost forever. Enjoy this as you descend, then meet Vermont Avenue and turn right. After only 100 feet or so, find your next staircase. This is Maryland Walk, and it's on the left. Drop down the many stages, all outfitted with good handrails on both sides, for a total of 72 steps. You land on Boynton.

Turn left and head down a slight grade on this divided road. In very short order, right after a big beige home on the left with exposed timbers, you will see a crosswalk. Take it, left and down the 11 steps to the downhill side of Boynton. Continue straight ahead to find your final staircase, and enter Boynton Walk.

Drop down 37 steps, broken into multiple sections, to land, at last, back on Arlington. Turn right and head uphill. Soon you will be in the shopping district, and back to your starting point.

ACKNOWLEDGMENTS

I required an enormous amount of help in the writing of this book, and I received it. When I reached out for collegial assistance, the Berkeley Path Wanderers Association and the Oakland Urban Paths reached back with enthusiasm. Without the BPWA's *A Map of Berkeley's Pathways* (and its counterpart, *Walk Oakland! Map & Guide*) I might not have started or finished the job of walking the East Bay stairs. I want particularly to thank Colleen Neff of the BWPA and Paul Rosenbloom of OUP for their support and encouragement.

I also needed an education in local history and design, and I received one from the Berkeley Architectural Heritage Association, whose *41 Berkeley Walking Tours* guide book, and online local architecture sites, are a treasure trove of historical data.

The walks themselves were tested by an army of local volunteers, without whose help this book would contain many errors. The *Secret Stairs: East Bay* test-walk team included: Colleen Neff, Cheryl Brewster, Gene Anderson, Tom Appleton and Doris Wurhmann, Ednah Beth Friedman, Ronna Benjamin, Lew Douglas, Carolyn Balling, Alison Monroe, Amy Katch, Denise Owen, David Schwartz, Buzz Cardoza, Rhoda Alvarez, Stephanie Gorevin, Martin and Nancy Thomas, Anat Razon, and Ellen Pasternack. I received guidance and local history from Bryce Nesbitt of the Kensington Improvement Club, and helpful local factoids, too, from author David S. Weinstein, Panoramic Hill Association member Richard White, and others. My Silver Lake stairwalking friend Steve Finkel provided excellent historical and factual assistance.

I also had the very good fortune to walk these walks in the company of very good friends. My Bay Area best pals Christopher Hall and Bruce McKenzie made me feel at home in their home. My transplanted Los Angeles friends Jennifer Grey and Eric Berkowitz let me drag them across the bay and up and down the Berkeley and Oakland hills. Rita Harowitz climbed the stairs in cowboy boots, and shot the beautiful photographs inside these pages. My daughter Katie Fleming blazed trails for me, bought me my first copy of *A Map of Berkeley's Pathways*, and kept me in good humor as we walked our first staircases together. And my wife Julie Singer walked with me, as she walks with me always.

INDEX